Better Homes and Gardens®

ENCYCLOPEDIA
of
COOKING

Volume 2

Strawberry Sunshine Pie is made in a pastry shell for a baked Alaska variation. The lemon sherbet and fresh strawberry filling stay cool while the fluffy meringue is browned.

On the cover: Beans come in a wide array of colors, shapes, and flavors to rank as one of the most popular vegetables. They are not only vegetables but also inexpensive meat substitutes.

BETTER HOMES AND GARDENS BOOKS
NEW YORK • DES MOINES

© Meredith Corporation, 1970, 1971, 1973. All Rights Reserved.
Printed in the United States of America.
Special Edition. Second Printing, 1973.
Library of Congress Catalog Card Number: 73-83173
SBN: 696-02022-X

BAGEL *(bā′ guhl)*—A handmade yeast roll twisted into a small doughnut shape. It is occasionally called a water doughnut.

The nonsweet dough is made with yeast, wheat flour, water, and sometimes eggs and onion. Bagels are simmered in water before they are baked giving the crust a glazed appearance. A bland flavor and chewy, white interior is typical of this roll.

Bagels are associated with Jewish cuisine and are often eaten with lox (smoked salmon) and cream cheese. (See *Bread, Jewish Cookery* for additional information.)

BAG PUDDING—A pudding made by wrapping dough in a floured cloth then cooking it in boiling water for several hours. There are two basic bag puddings: a dessert pudding made with fruit such as berries and a main dish pudding which contains a meat mixture enclosed in a doughy crust.

BAGUETTE *(ba get′)*—A rod-shaped French bread. This long cylindrical loaf is about two feet long yet quite small in diameter. The bread is notable for its thick, crisp, golden crust. (See also *French Bread.*)

BAIN-MARIE *(ban′ muh rē′)*—A French utensil similar to a double boiler. A pan containing the food is set into a larger pan or casserole, half filled with hot water. Because the two pans do not fit together as a double boiler does, the water remains near the boiling point but does not boil over or steam. A larger version of the bain-marie that resembles a steam table, has several openings for pots or pans with hot water or steam circulating around and under the food containers.

The bain-marie is used to cook delicate dishes such as custards, puddings, mousses, and fish or meat loaves. This method of cooking without direct heat prevents the food from curdling or disintegrating.

The bain-marie may also be used, as is the double boiler—to keep food warm. Purée, béarnaise, hollandaise, allemande, and white or brown gravy can be kept hot while retaining the eating quality.

The literal translation of bain-marie is "bath of Maria" but the translation "water bath" is the most appropriate in reference to food preparation.

BAKE—To cook by dry heat, covered or uncovered, in an oven or oven-type appliance, under coals, or on heated metal or stone. Cooking meat uncovered is called roasting except for ham which is baked.

Oven Chart	
Very slow oven	250°-275°
Slow oven	300°-325°
Moderate oven	350°-375°
Hot oven	400°-425°
Very hot oven	450°-475°
Extremely hot oven	500°-525°

BAKED ALASKA—A dessert made with cake and ice cream covered with meringue and baked or broiled until the meringue is golden. The ice cream will remain firm.

The origin of this glamorous dessert dates back to the early 1800s when it was first known as Alaska-Florida, presumedly because of the contrasting cold and hot nature of the ingredients. The name "baked Alaska" has now been adopted.

The dessert is made from a cake layer which is at least one inch thick and should extend one half to one inch beyond the ice cream edges. Sherbet or a combination of ice cream or sherbet flavors can be used as well as ice cream. A soft meringue is spread thickly and completely over the ice cream and cake. It's extremely important that the meringue meets the edges of the cake to form a seal all around the ice cream. The alaska is baked in a very hot oven or broiled until the meringue is browned.

Tiny air cells in the meringue act as an insulator to keep the heat away from the ice cream, but once cut baked Alaska must be served quickly because the warmth of the room air will melt the ice cream.

The classic baked Alaska of cake, ice cream, and meringue has many modern variations. Individual servings are made by putting the ice cream into hollowed out cupcakes or orange shells. Or, for pie lovers the ice cream can even be put into a pastry shell. Some other variations include fruit under the meringue cover.

To save last-minute preparation of any of the Alaska recipes (classic or variation), the baked Alaska can be assembled completely on a wooden cutting board, wrapped, and frozen several days ahead. At serving time, just whisk the Alaska into a preheated oven to brown the meringue and the elegant dessert is ready to serve with little bother. (See *Dessert, Ice Cream, Meringue* for additional information.)

Orange Alaskas

Dieter's will love this low-calorie dessert at only 111 calories per serving—

    4 small oranges
    ½ cup frozen whipped dessert
        topping, thawed
    1 egg white
    ⅛ teaspoon cream of tartar
    ⅛ teaspoon vanilla
    1 tablespoon sugar
    1 egg yolk

Cut a thin slice off bottom of each orange to make it sit flat. Cut off tops of oranges a fourth of the way down. Remove tops and discard. Carefully scoop out pulp, reserving pulp, juice, and shells; discard seeds. Place orange pulp and orange juice in blender container. Cover; blend till pureed. Stir in whipped dessert topping. Pour into 2-cup freezer tray; freeze the mixture till firm.

Just before serving, beat egg white with cream of tartar and vanilla till soft peaks form; gradually add sugar, beating till stiff peaks form. In a separate bowl, thoroughly beat egg yolk. Gently fold beaten egg yolk into stiffly beaten egg white mixture.

Break up frozen orange mixture and spoon into orange shells. Cover with meringue mixture, sealing to edges of oranges all around. Bake at 500° till lightly browned, about 2 to 3 minutes. Makes 4 servings.

Do a magic trick

←Serve hot and cold Mile-High Mocha Alaska right from the oven. Everyone will be convinced a magician has performed this feat.

Strawberry Sunshine Pie

    Plain Pastry for 1 9-inch crust
        (See *Pastry*)
    1 pint lemon sherbet, softened
    3 egg whites
    ½ teaspoon vanilla
    ¼ teaspoon cream of tartar
    7 tablespoons sugar
    1 quart fresh strawberries,
        sliced

Prepare Plain Pastry according to recipe directions. Fit pastry into 9-inch pie plate trimming ½ to 1 inch beyond edge. Fold under and flute edge of pastry. Bake at 450° for 10 to 12 minutes or till golden. Cool completely.

Spread sherbet in bottom of pastry shell; freeze till firm, 4 to 5 hours or overnight. Beat egg whites with vanilla and cream of tartar till soft peaks form. Gradually add *6 tablespoons* sugar, beating till stiff and glossy peaks form.

Sweeten strawberries with remaining sugar. Working quickly, arrange strawberries over lemon sherbet. Spread meringue over berries being careful to seal meringue to edge of pastry.

Place pie on cutting board and bake at 475° for 5 to 6 minutes or till meringue is golden. Cut in wedges with sharp knife dipped in water. Serve immediately. Makes 6 to 8 servings.

Cupcake Alaska

    4 large chocolate cupcakes
    2 egg whites
    ⅛ teaspoon cream of tartar
    ¼ teaspoon vanilla
      Dash salt
    ¼ cup sugar
      Ice cream (butter brickle, pistachio,
        butter pecan, or cherry-nut)

Hollow out center of cupcakes, leaving about ¼-inch of cake around sides and bottom. Beat egg whites with cream of tartar, vanilla, and salt till soft peaks form. Gradually add sugar, beating to stiff peaks. Fill cupcakes with ice cream and place on wooden cutting board. Quickly cover top and sides with meringue, sealing edges at bottom. Place Alaskas in freezer. At serving time, bake Alaskas at 500° till meringue is browned, 2 to 3 minutes. Serve immediately. Makes 4 servings.

Spread plenty of meringue around the edge where ice cream and cake meet. This seal keeps the ice cream firm while being baked.

Mile-High Mocha Alaska

        2 pints chocolate ice cream
        1 to 2 pints coffee ice cream
        1 Brownie Layer
        5 egg whites
       ⅔ cup sugar

For a mold, line deep 1½-quart bowl with foil, allowing 1 inch extra to extend over edge of bowl. Stir chocolate ice cream to soften, *slightly;* using back of spoon spread a layer about 1 inch thick over bottom and sides of foil liner. Place mold in freezer. Stir coffee ice cream to soften *slightly*. Remove mold from freezer. Pack coffee ice cream into center of mold. Cover with foil, pressing to smooth top. Freeze till *firm*.

For Brownie Layer, prepare one recipe Cake Brownies (See *Brownie*), baking in greased 8-inch *round* pan. Cool; remove from pan.

To assemble Alaska, place cooled Brownie Layer on cookie sheet or wooden cutting board. Let ice cream mold stand at room temperature to loosen from sides while preparing meringue.

Beat egg whites till soft peaks form; gradually add sugar, beating till stiff peaks form. Remove foil from top of ice cream; invert ice cream mold onto Brownie Layer. Lift off bowl and peel foil off the ice cream mold.

Working quickly cover ice cream mold and Brownie Layer with meringue. Swirl meringue into peaks and seal around edges of cake.

Place cookie sheet or wooden board on lowest rack in oven at once and bake at 500° for 3 minutes or till meringue is golden brown. Let stand a few minutes for easier cutting. Cut in wedge-shaped slices. Serves 12.

Baked Alaska

        1 1-inch layer sponge *or* layer
            cake
        1 quart brick of ice cream *or*
            2 pint bricks ice cream
        5 egg whites
       ⅔ cup sugar
            Sugar

Trim cake 1-inch larger on all sides than brick ice cream; place cake on wooden cutting board. (Keep ice cream frozen.) Beat egg whites till soft peaks form; gradually add ⅔ cup sugar, beating till stiff peaks form.

Center brick of ice cream on cake layer (place pints side-by-side if used). Spread meringue over ice cream and cake, sealing to edges of cake all around. Swirl in peaks. Sprinkle lightly with sugar. Bake at 500° till meringue is golden, about 3 minutes. Slice and serve immediately. Makes 8 servings.

BAKERS' CHEESE—A skim milk cheese resembling cottage cheese but softer in texture and sharper in flavor. It is used primarily in commercial baking of cheese cakes and pastries. (See also *Cheese.*)

BAKING DISH—A glass or ceramic utensil capable of withstanding oven temperatures. Shapes vary from casseroles to shallow dishes. Sizes are measured in inches or quarts; always use exact size specified.

Because glass and ceramic hold more heat than metal does, the oven temperature should be lowered 25 degrees when using glass and ceramic dishes where the recipe does not specify glass. (See also *Pots and Pans.*)

BAKING PAN—A metal utensil used for oven cooking made of lightweight aluminum or stainless steel. A good baking pan should cook food evenly and thoroughly. (See also *Pots and Pans.*)

BAKING POWDER—A chemical leavening consisting of a mixture of an acid-reacting material and sodium bicarbonate (baking soda). A starch, usually cornstarch, is added to standardize the mixture and keep it dry. This prevents the acid and soda from reacting with each other in the can.

When liquid and baking powder are mixed in the preparation of baked foods, carbon dioxide gas bubbles are trapped in the mixture. This causes the dough to rise and to become light and porous. The heat applied during baking is necessary to stabilize this porous structure.

Although this principle of leavening by using baking soda with an acid salt was familiar to homemakers before baking powder was on the retail market, the leavening of baked foods was a hit or miss affair. Homemakers talked of either having good luck or poor luck with the week's baking. There is little science, however, to their theory of luck. Failures were more likely caused by improper leavening than luck. Variations in measuring the amount of baking soda and cream of tartar used in the recipe, or leaving the measurement to guesswork were more often the cause of the poor baked products.

Although the first formulas for baking powder were developed in the United States in the 1850s, it seems unlikely, because of poor transportation facilities, that baking powder was widely available in the United States until after the Civil War. Early baking powder formulas included various acids mixed with baking soda and starch or flour. Sometimes the baking soda and the acid were packaged in separate containers and accompanied by instructions and a wooden measuring device.

Types of baking powder: There are four types of baking powder: tartrate, phosphate, anhydrous phosphate, and sodium aluminum sulfate-phosphate. All four types contain a starch and baking soda but the acid salt ingredient differs.

Tartrate baking powders contain the acid ingredients cream of tartar and tartaric acid. The first baking powders sold were this type. These baking powders are known as single-action because they are quick to react as soon as moistened. Much of the gas is given off during mixing and the remainder is released during baking. Because all of this happens as a continuous reaction, speedy handling of the batter from bowl to oven is essential so that as much of the rising action as possible takes place in the oven.

Phosphate baking powders contain calcium or sodium phosphate as the acid salt. These release a fair amount (but not as much as tartrate baking powders) of the carbon dioxide in the cold mixture. The rest is released during baking.

Anhydrous phosphate baking powders have anhydrous monocalcium phosphate as their acid ingredient. This acid salt has been treated to slow down the rate at which it dissolves. Little carbon dioxide is released during mixing. Carbon dioxide production accelerates early in the baking period. This type of baking powder is not sold extensively on the retail market but is widely used in packaged mixes.

Sodium aluminum sulfate-phosphate baking powders contain sodium aluminum sulfate and calcium phosphate, as acid salts. Since sodium aluminum sulfate reacts slowly with baking soda, the phosphate is added to speed up the reaction.

Baking powders of this type are considered double-action because the phosphate reacts with the baking soda while the mixture is cold, whereas heat is necessary before the sulfate reacts. About 85 percent of baking powders sold on the retail market are sodium aluminum sulfate-phosphate.

Unless another type of baking powder is specified, a double-action product is intended in most recipes.

Baking powder is a small ingredient in a recipe yet it has great influence on the shape, volume, grain, texture, and lightness of the finished product.

Accurate level measurement of baking powder is very important. The exact amount a recipe calls for gives the product the best texture and volume. Too little baking powder makes baked foods heavy and compact. Too much can cause over-rising followed by collapse, coarse loose texture, and often a lingering baking powder taste. As a general guide, one to two teaspoons of baking powder should be used for every cup of flour in a recipe.

Orange Celebration Cake

⅓ cup butter or margarine
⅓ cup shortening
2 teaspoons grated orange peel
1½ cups sugar
3 eggs
2½ cups sifted cake flour
2½ teaspoons baking powder
1 teaspoon salt
1 cup orange juice
Orange Filling
Seven Minute Frosting (See
Frosting for recipe)

Cream together butter, shortening, and peel. Gradually add sugar, creaming till light. Add eggs, one at a time, beating well after each. Sift together dry ingredients and add alternately with orange juice to creamed mixture, beating after each addition. Bake in 2 greased and lightly floured 9x1½-inch round pans at 350° for 25 to 30 minutes or till done. Cool 10 minutes; remove from pans. Cool.

Fill layers with *Orange Filling:* Combine ⅔ cup sugar and 3 tablespoons all-purpose flour in saucepan. Add 1 cup orange juice and 2 egg yolks. Cook and stir till mixture boils; cook 1 minute. Stir in 2 tablespoons butter; cool. Frost cake with Seven Minute Frosting.

Onion Biscuits

¼ cup finely chopped onion
1 tablespoon shortening
1½ cups sifted all-purpose flour
1½ teaspoons baking powder
½ teaspoon celery seed
¼ cup shortening
1 slightly beaten egg
⅓ cup milk

Cook onion in 1 tablespoon shortening till tender. Sift together flour, baking powder, and ½ teaspoon salt; stir in celery seed. Cut in shortening till mixture resembles coarse crumbs. Add onion, egg, and milk all at once and stir just till dough follows fork around bowl.

Turn out on lightly floured surface and knead gently ½ minute. Pat or roll ½ inch thick. Cut with floured 1¾-inch cutter. Bake on ungreased baking sheet at 425° for 12 minutes or till done. Makes 12 biscuits.

Since baking powder was first introduced in the middle of the 19th century, housewives have found it more convenient and reliable than baking soda alone. Today most recipes, though by no means all, use baking powder or baking powder plus additional soda in place of baking soda by itself. (See also *Leavening Agent.*)

BAKING SODA—Pure sodium bicarbonate. Chemical leavening is almost universally produced by carbon dioxide gas resulting from the reaction of sodium bicarbonate (baking soda) with an acid.

When sodium bicarbonate is heated, it gives off carbon dioxide gas and leaves sodium carbonate. In baked foods this compound has an objectionable taste which is eliminated by combining the baking soda with an acid at the time the batter is mixed. This acid ingredient can be present in the food or in the baking powder.

Soured milk, buttermilk, sour cream, molasses, vinegar, and fruit juices are some of the acid-containing foods used with baking soda in baking. Since the acidity of these foods varies, it is difficult to know how much baking soda to add. Baking powder contains a standardized amount of baking soda and acid salt so takes much of the guesswork out of baking.

If the carbon dioxide evolved by the reaction of an acid food and baking soda is to be used for leavening, the soda must be sifted with the dry ingredients. If it is mixed with the acid ingredient before adding, the gas will be lost.

A pinch of baking soda is sometimes suggested as a means of keeping green vegetables green as they cook or of making dried beans tender more quickly. Nutritionists frown on this practice, however, because it hastens the loss of thiamine and makes the vegetables mushy.

Baking soda is used in various types of chocolate cake because of the way in which it affects the brown color. The most soda is used in Devil's food cake, giving it a rich mahogany color when soured milk is an ingredient or a deep red when sweet milk is used, instead. The use of baking soda in any type of chocolate cake results in a cake that is darker than one made with all baking powder.

Prize Chocolate Cake

⅔ cup shortening
1¼ cups sugar
1½ teaspoons vanilla
3 1-ounce squares unsweetened
    chocolate, melted and cooled
3 eggs
1½ cups sifted all-purpose flour
¾ teaspoon baking soda
¾ teaspoon salt
1¼ cups sour milk *or* buttermilk

Cream shortening and sugar till light and fluffy. Blend in vanilla and cooled chocolate. Add eggs, one at a time, beating well after each addition. Sift together flour, baking soda, and salt; add to creamed mixture alternately with milk, beating after each addition. Bake in greased and lightly-floured 13x9x2-inch baking pan at 350° for 35 to 40 minutes or till done. Cool. Frost.

Spiced Chocolate Cake

⅔ cup shortening
2 cups sifted all-purpose flour
2 cups sugar
1 teaspoon baking powder
1 teaspoon baking soda
1 teaspoon salt
1 teaspoon ground cloves
1 teaspoon ground cinnamon
1 teaspoon instant coffee powder
1½ cups buttermilk
3 eggs
4 1-ounce squares unsweetened
    chocolate, melted and cooled
1 teaspoon vanilla
    Seven Minute Frosting (See
    Frosting for recipe)

Place shortening in mixing bowl. Sift in flour, sugar, baking powder, baking soda, salt, ground cloves, ground cinnamon, and instant coffee powder. Add *1 cup* of the buttermilk; mix till all flour is moistened. Beat mixture vigorously 2 minutes.

Stir in remaining buttermilk, eggs, cooled chocolate, and vanilla. Beat 2 minutes longer. Bake in greased and lightly floured 13x9x2-inch baking dish at 350° for 40 minutes or till done. Cool. Frost with Seven Minute Frosting.

Butterscotch Cookies

½ cup butter or margarine
⅔ cup brown sugar
1 egg
1⅓ cups sifted all-purpose
    flour
¾ teaspoon baking soda
¾ teaspoon vanilla
⅓ cup chopped walnuts

Melt butter in 2-quart saucepan; add sugar and mix well. Add egg; beat till light colored. Sift flour with baking soda; stir into egg mixture. Add vanilla and walnuts. Chill.

Roll into small balls. Bake on ungreased cookie sheet at 375° for 7 to 10 minutes. Remove from cookie sheet at once. Makes 3 dozen.

Aside from its baking properties, sodium bicarbonate is a versatile cleansing agent. Many people use it instead of a commercial toothpaste. Soda is also used to clean painted walls, plastic tablecloths, windows, costume jewelry, and fine crystal. Baking soda will rid hands of fishy odors, take the soreness out of sunburn, clear refrigerators of stale odors, and sooth the itch or sting of insect bites. (See also *Leavening Agent.*)

BAKLAVA, BAKALAWA *(bä′ kluh vä)*—A Greek and Middle Eastern dessert made of wafer-thin pastry sheets filled with nuts, butter, and honey, and covered with honey or a sugar syrup. These pastries are usually cut into diamond-shaped pieces for serving. (See also *Greek Cookery.*)

BALM—Any of various aromatic plants similar to mint. Lemon balm is the best known variety and the word balm usually refers to this herb.

Lemon balm is a hardy perennial herb which reaches a height of 1½ to 2 feet. It has broad, dark green, crinkled leaves, which have a fragrant lemon odor and a faint lemon flavor. The pale yellow flowers grow in clusters. Lemon balm thrives in all temperate climates and is often used as an attractive garden border.

The ancient Greeks and Orientals crushed lemon balm and used it to flavor their tea and wine drinks. Tea made from balm leaves was valued by the Arabs because it made "the heart merry and joyful."

Many medicinal properties have been attributed to this herb. In ancient Greece, balm leaves were used in medicinal drinks as remedies for scorpion or dog bites. The leaves were also applied to the body to relieve the pain of gout, draw out congestion, and "leave one light-headed." In some European countries, fresh balm leaves are still used as a remedy for fainting and virus cold fevers.

Although the leaves and tender sprigs lend a subtle, charming lemon flavor to lemonade, teas, meats, poultry, sauces, stuffings, soups, and salads, the use of lemon balm has declined in the United States. This decline is possibly due to the year round availability of lemons. Today the prime use of balm is in the industrial manufacture of perfumes and liqueurs. (See also *Herbs*.)

BAMBOO SHOOT—The edible young sprout from certain varieties of the tropical plant, bamboo. Since only the young shoots are tender, bamboo shoots must be harvested before they become mature. To keep the shoots tender and fit for consumption longer, the young plants are covered with hills of earth. The shoots are then cut as soon as the tiny tip appears through the top of the mound.

Although the supply is more abundant in autumn, bamboo shoots are harvested the year round. Each shoot is covered with a thick, tight, overlapping, spiny sheath that must be stripped off before the succulent inner flesh of the bamboo shoot can be cooked and eaten.

In the Orient where they grow, bamboo shoots are used as a vegetable and served similar to asparagus. Bamboo shoots are also salted and eaten with rice; pickled; candied; and used in meat dishes.

Fresh bamboo shoots are available only near the growing area, but cooked, canned shoots are imported from Taiwan and Japan and are available in markets in this country. These shoots have a flavor somewhat resembling the flavor of artichokes and are most frequently used as an ingredient in oriental dishes.

Chicken Almond

> 2 **cups skinned uncooked chicken breasts cut in thin strips (about 2 whole breasts)**
> ¼ **cup shortening or salad oil**
> 3 **cups chicken broth**
> 2 **5-ounce cans bamboo shoots, drained and diced**
> 2 **5-ounce cans water chestnuts, drained and sliced**
> 2 **cups diced celery**
> 1 **cup diced bok choy (Chinese chard) *or* romaine**
> 2 **tablespoons soy sauce**
> 2 **teaspoons monosodium glutamate**
> ⅓ **cup cornstarch**
> ½ **cup cold water**
> ½ **cup halved almonds, toasted**
>
> • • •
>
> **Hot cooked rice**

In large heavy skillet quickly cook chicken in hot shortening or salad oil. Add chicken broth, bamboo shoots, water chestnuts, celery, bok choy *or* romaine, soy sauce, and monosodium glutamate; mix thoroughly. Bring to boiling; cover and cook over low heat for 5 minutes. Vegetables should be tender yet still crisp.

Blend cornstarch and cold water; add to chicken mixture. Cook, stirring constantly, till mixture thickens and bubbles. Salt to taste. Garnish with almonds. Serve immediately over hot cooked rice. Makes 6 servings.

Note: High heat and quick stirring are essential; avoid overcooking.

If part of a can is leftover, bamboo shoots can be kept for quite awhile in the refrigerator. To store leftovers, place the shoots in a clean container, cover them with cold water, and seal the container with an airtight lid. Place the leftovers in the warmest part of the refrigerator and change the water at least every other day. (See also *Oriental Cookery*.)

BAMBOO SKEWERS—Slender sticks, made from slivered bamboo. These skewers vary in length from 4 to 10 inches and are popularly used for the hibachi cooking of kebabs. Food strung on the bamboo skewers are rotated over the hibachi coals.

BANANA

BANANA—The elongated yellow- or red-rinded fruit of the tropical banana plant. These popular fruits, like many other foods, have been eating favorites for thousands of years. In fact, history suggests that bananas were one of the very first plants to be cultivated by man. The evidence indicates they were known in southern Asia during prehistoric times and, in all likelihood, probably originated in the East Indies. Bananas were also cultivated in India some 4,000 years ago.

Two ancient names for the banana give an indication of the esteem in which the fruit was held. One name translates as "fruit of the wise man" and another means the "fruit of paradise."

Explorers and traders are credited with carrying banana plants to the Near East and to Africa. Spanish missionaries then introduced them to the tropical Americas after Columbus made his voyages and discovered the banana in that area.

The two-fruit combination in Strawberry-Banana Mold has long been a refreshing favorite with children and adults alike.

How bananas are produced: Although banana plants resemble trees, they are, nevertheless, plants with trunk-like stems made of leafstalks wrapped tightly together in long, stiff bundles. At maturity (12 to 15 months), the plants have grown to a height of from 10 to 18 feet. The plant loaded with fruit is an interesting sight because the fruit appears to grow upside down.

Bananas prefer loose, well-drained soil and humid, tropical weather. Thus the bananas purchased in American markets all year are imported from plantations in tropical countries, mainly Central America, South America, and the West Indies where they are an important crop.

Unlike most fruits, bananas are harvested in bunches when mature but still green since flavor decreases as a banana ripens on the tree. Once picked, the fruit or "hands" are removed from the bunch, broken into clusters, and packed in fiberboard cartons. While on board the cargo ships the bananas are stored in atmospherically controlled rooms.

Similar handling care and storage control protect the quality of the fruit as it is transported across the United States. Upon reaching final destination, the fruit is placed in ripening rooms which have scientifically-controlled moisture content and temperature. During ripening under these conditions much of the starch in the bananas is changed to sugar.

Nutritional value: About one-fourth of the bananas' food value is in the form of carbohydrates, mainly sugar. Bananas contain vitamins A and C plus all of the B vitamin group. One 6-inch banana contains about 85 calories.

Types of bananas: Some 300 varieties of banana exist but three main types are commonly marketed. Two of these are eaten and used like other fruits. The yellow, smooth-skinned banana is the type most frequently seen in grocery stores. Red banana, a lesser-known variety, is shorter and thicker than the yellow one, but has similar flavor and texture.

Plantain, the third type, resembles the yellow banana in shape and color but is thicker and larger. The hard, starchy plantain however, is eaten as a cooked vegetable rather than as a fruit. It is a staple in Central American kitchens.

How to select: Choosing good bananas requires familiarization with the bananas themselves and their popularity with your family. Special terminology, for instance, describes bananas as seen in markets.

A bunch of bananas is the whole growth of fruit as picked from the plant, while a hand of bananas is a natural grouping of 6 to 15 bananas within the bunch. The bananas on the market today come in clusters or partial hands rather than full bunches as in the past. Most stores sell the fruit on a price-per-pound basis.

An individual banana is called a finger. Its neck is the part attached to the crown. The tip of the banana, usually the last part to lose its green color as the fruit ripens, is the unattached or blossom end.

Buy bananas by the cluster that are not quite full yellow in color. Single bananas have been pulled away from the crown; they are more likely to be bruised or cracked than those in natural groupings.

Buy in relation to menu plans and family eating habits. As an added guide, about two or three medium bananas are in one pound. One pound of unpeeled bananas yields 2 cups sliced or 1½ cups mashed.

How to store: Bananas ripen to full flavor and soft smooth texture very easily at room temperature. To prevent bruises or decay, leave them attached to the crown until ready to use them. When the desired stage of ripening has been reached, bananas can be stored in the refrigerator several days to retard overripening. The skins will darken, but the flavor and texture of the fruit remain unchanged.

How to prepare: The bananas' degree of coloration is a key to how they may best be used. Underripe ones, which appear mostly yellow with a little green on neck and tip, are slightly tart in flavor and have firm, starchy pulp. When baked, broiled, sautéed, or fried, their delicious flavor is enhanced. These underripe fruit are also preferred by some people for out-of-hand eating or for salads.

Broiler Banana Splits

    2 medium bananas
      Lemon juice
  ¼ cup butter or margarine
  ½ cup brown sugar
    2 tablespoons light cream
  ½ cup corn flakes
      Vanilla ice cream

Peel bananas; split in half lengthwise, then in half crosswise. Place in shallow pan. Brush with lemon juice. In saucepan melt butter; stir in sugar and cream. Cook and stir till bubbly. Remove from heat; add cornflakes. Spoon over bananas.

Broil 5 inches from heat till bubbly (about 2 minutes). Spoon into dishes; top with scoops of ice cream. Makes 4 servings.

Ripe bananas completely yellow in color are ready for any use. Fully ripe bananas have deep yellow peels with brown flecks and are perfect in flavor and texture for eating with cereals, in salads or desserts. These latter bananas can be mashed easily with a fork or rotary beater, or puréed by pushing slices through a strainer.

Banana Ice Cream

  ¾ cup sugar
  1½ teaspoons unflavored gelatin
  ¾ cup light cream
    2 fully-ripe medium bananas,
        mashed (1 cup)
    2 well-beaten egg yolks
    2 teaspoons lemon juice
    1 teaspoon vanilla
    2 cups whipping cream
    2 egg whites

Combine ½ cup sugar, gelatin, and ¼ teaspoon salt in saucepan. Stir in light cream. Stir over low heat till gelatin and sugar are dissolved. Chill till partially set.

Blend in banana, yolks, lemon juice, and vanilla. Whip cream; fold into gelatin. Beat egg whites to soft peaks. Gradually add remaining sugar beating to stiff peaks. Fold into banana mixture. Pour into large freezer tray. Freeze firm. Makes 2 quarts.

If cut slices are not to be used immediately, remember to brush the peeled and sliced bananas with ascorbic acid color keeper or lemon juice mixed with a little water to prevent darkening.

How to use: Bananas belong with main dishes as meat accompaniments when glazed or fried; in quick breads, in cakes, cookies, pies, and puddings; in ice cream, sherbet, or other frozen desserts; in milk shakes or nogs; in sauces and toppings; and in salads and some sandwiches. But still most popular of all are the bananas which are peeled and eaten out-of-hand. (See also *Fruit.*)

Strawberry-Banana Mold

> 2 3-ounce packages strawberry-
>   flavored gelatin
> 2 cups boiling water
> 1 10-ounce package frozen
>   strawberries
> 1 cup cold water
>   • • •
> 2 medium bananas
> 1 cup whipping cream

Dissolve gelatin in boiling water. Thaw berries *just enough* to drain off 1 tablespoon syrup; reserve the 1 tablespoon syrup. Add berries to gelatin; break in small chunks with fork then stir to completely thaw berries. Add cold water. Chill till partially set.

Peel bananas. Slice bananas on the bias into gelatin; stir gently to distribute fruit. Pour into 6½-cup fluted mold. Chill till firm; unmold. If desired, garnish with greens and additional bias-cut banana slices dipped in ascorbic acid color keeper to retain color.

Top with *Strawberry Whipped Cream:* Whip cream to soft peaks. Stir reserved strawberry syrup into cream. Makes 8 to 10 servings.

Nut-Crusted Bananas

Peel fully ripe bananas. Cut in half crosswise and then in half lengthwise. Dip in a mixture of equal parts honey and lime juice. Arrange on plate and sprinkle generously with chopped macadamia nuts or walnuts.

Banana Ambrosia Ring

Mix ½ cup flaked coconut; ⅓ cup maple-flavored syrup; and 2 tablespoons butter or margarine, melted. Spread over bottom of 6½-cup ring mold. Combine 2 cups packaged biscuit mix and 3 tablespoons sugar. Stir in 1 banana, mashed (½ cup); 1 slightly beaten egg; and 3 tablespoons butter or margarine, melted.

Beat mixture vigorously for 1 minute. Spoon *half* the batter over coconut in mold. Mix 2 tablespoons sugar with 2 tablespoons butter or margarine, softened, and 1 teaspoon ground cinnamon; sprinkle over batter in mold. Cover with remaining batter. Bake at 375° for 20 minutes or till done. Invert to unmold. Serve warm. Makes 6 to 8 servings.

Banana Fritters

> 5 to 6 firm medium bananas
> 2 tablespoons orange juice
> 1 tablespoon sugar
> 1 cup sifted all-purpose flour
> ½ teaspoon baking powder
> ¼ teaspoon salt
> ¾ cup milk
> 1 slightly beaten egg
> 2 tablespoons butter or margarine,
>   melted
> 1 teaspoon grated orange peel
> ¼ teaspoon vanilla
>   Orange-Lemon Sauce

Peel bananas; cut in 3-inch pieces then halve lengthwise. Let stand in mixture of orange juice and sugar. Sift together flour, baking powder, and salt. Combine next 5 ingredients; add to flour mixture, stirring only till moistened. Drain bananas; dip into batter, spreading batter evenly over bananas.

Fry in deep hot fat (375°) for 2 to 3 minutes or till fritters are golden brown; drain. Serve with whipped cream, if desired. Pass Orange-Lemon Sauce. Makes 6 to 8 servings.

Orange-Lemon Sauce: Combine ½ cup sugar, 1½ tablespoons cornstarch, and dash salt in saucepan; stir in ¾ cup water. Bring mixture to boiling, stirring constantly. Cook and stir till thickened and bubbly. Remove sauce from heat; add ¼ cup orange juice, 2 tablespoons butter or margarine, and 1 tablespoon lemon juice. Serve warm. Makes 1⅓ cups sauce.

Banana Burgers

    1 beaten egg
    ¼ teaspoon ground cinnamon
    1 pound ground beef
    1 small banana
    4 frankfurter buns, split and
       toasted

Combine egg, 1 teaspoon salt, and cinnamon. Add meat; mix well. Peel banana; cut in half crosswise, then in half lengthwise. Divide meat into 4 portions; shape each portion around banana quarter. Broil 3 inches from heat for 12 minutes, turning ¼ turn every 3 minutes. Serve in buns. Makes 4 servings.

Banana Cream Pie

    Plain Pastry for 1-crust 9-inch pie
      (See *Pastry*)
    ¾ cup sugar
    ⅓ cup all-purpose flour *or*
       3 tablespoons cornstarch
    2 cups milk
    3 slightly beaten egg yolks
    2 tablespoons butter or margarine
    1 teaspoon vanilla
    3 ripe medium bananas
    Soft Meringue

Fit rolled Plain Pastry into 9-inch pie plate; flute edges. Prick bottom and sides well with fork. Bake at 450° for 10 to 12 minutes or till golden; cool thoroughly.

    Meanwhile, in saucepan combine sugar, flour, and ¼ teaspoon salt; gradually stir in milk. Cook and stir till mixture is thick and bubbly. Cook and stir 2 minutes longer. Remove from heat. Stir small amount of hot mixture into yolks; immediately return to hot mixture. Cook 2 minutes, stirring constantly.

    Remove from heat. Add butter and vanilla. Peel bananas; slice into cooled baked pastry shell. Pour pudding over. Spread Soft Meringue on top, sealing to pastry. Bake at 350° about 12 to 15 minutes, or till meringue is golden. Cool pie before cutting.

    Soft Meringue: Beat 3 egg whites with ½ teaspoon vanilla and ¼ teaspoon cream of tartar till soft peaks form. Gradually add 6 tablespoons sugar, beating till stiff peaks form and all sugar is dissolved.

Bananas Foster

Peel 6 large ripe bananas and halve lengthwise, brush with lemon juice. In skillet melt ¾ cup brown sugar and 6 tablespoons butter. Add bananas; cook till almost tender, about 3 minutes. Drizzle ¼ cup orange liqueur atop. Serve with ice cream. Makes 6 servings.

Banana Pecan Crunch

    2 tablespoons butter or margarine
    6 medium bananas, peeled and
       sliced crosswise
    ½ cup broken pecans
    2 tablespoons molasses
    ½ cup brown sugar
    2 tablespoons butter or margarine,
       melted

In 11x7x1½-inch baking pan melt the first 2 tablespoons butter; layer bananas and nuts in pan. Drizzle with molasses. Sprinkle brown sugar and melted butter over. Bake at 350° for 10 minutes. Makes 6 servings.

Bubbling Bananas Foster can be an elegant prepare-at-the-table dessert. Serve as is or with scoops of vanilla ice cream.

BANANA FLAKES—Dehydrated, ripe banana in the form of small thin flakes. When re-hydrated into mashed banana, banana flakes can be used for infant and invalid feeding. After adding the proper amount of liquid to them, they also can be used as an ingredient in some recipes calling for a specific measure of mashed banana.

BANANA FLOUR—Thoroughly dried, ripe banana finely ground into a nutritious and easily digestible meal. It is white to very pale yellow in color and has a pleasing taste and slightly fruity aroma. Banana flour was designed primarily for use in a semiliquid food served to invalids.

BANANA PEPPER—A slender yellow pepper, usually pickled, that is popular in Italian cuisine as a relish or antipasto ingredient. Banana peppers are primarily marketed in jars and are seldom found fresh on produce counters except in areas where they are grown. (See also *Pepper*.)

BANANA SQUASH—A cylindrical, banana-shaped vegetable of the gourd family. This variety of squash is most frequently served on the Pacific Coast.

In appearance, the outer skin of banana squash is smooth and light greenish-gray to creamy pink in color. Some can grow to a length of 2 feet and weigh 12 pounds. The outer shell is thin and hard. When cooked, the light orange, edible flesh is fine grained, of good flavor, and moderately dry.

Cooking techniques used for banana squash are similar to those used for other winter squash varieties. (See *Squash, Winter Squash* for additional information.)

Baked Banana Squash

   1 3-pound banana squash
½ cup brown sugar
¼ cup butter or margarine,
    softened
   1 teaspoon paprika

Cut squash into serving pieces; remove seeds. Place skin side up in baking dish; pour ⅓ cup hot water in dish. Bake 20 minutes at 375°.

Turn squash skin side down. Combine brown sugar, butter, and paprika; spread over squash. Continue baking about 5 to 10 minutes or till squash is tender, basting frequently to glaze. To serve, pass extra butter. Makes 8 servings.

BANBURY TART—A square-, triangular-, round-, or half-moon-shaped pastry with a tart-sweet filling of raisins and currants. These pies in miniature were named after the city of Banbury, England. The name is sometimes given to short, filled cookies or bars with similar filling. (See *English Cookery, Tart* for additional information.)

Banbury Tarts

¼ cup sugar
  1 teaspoon cornstarch
¼ teaspoon ground cinnamon
¼ teaspoon ground nutmeg
½ cup water
  1 teaspoon grated lemon peel
  1 tablespoon lemon juice
  1 cup raisins
   Plain Pastry for 2-crust 9-inch
    pie (See *Pastry*)
   Milk *or* egg yolk

In saucepan, blend sugar, cornstarch, cinnamon, and nutmeg. Stir in water, lemon peel and juice; add raisins. Cook and stir till thickened and bubbly; cool.

Cut rolled Plain Pastry into twelve 5-inch circles. Place about 1 tablespoon raisin mixture on half of each pastry round. Moisten edges; fold over and press together with a fork. Brush with milk or slightly beaten egg yolk. Cut slit in top to permit steam to escape. Place tarts on cookie sheet. Bake at 350° for 25 to 30 minutes or till browned.

BANNOCK *(ban' uhk)*—An oatmeal, wheat meal, or barley hearth bread popular in Scotland and England. Modern-day bannocks are usually baked on a griddle instead of before open hearths or fires as was done in years past. The Scottish people serve bannocks as frequently as biscuits are served in the southern United States. (See also *English Cookery*.)

BARBECUE

*A guide to fire building, equipment, and cooking
—designed to increase barbecuing pleasure.*

A familiar word in almost every household, barbecue has developed several meanings over the years. 1. Cooking meat and other foods over an open fire. 2. An outdoor party or gathering at which foods prepared over an open fire are served. 3. Equipment used in preparing foods over an open fire such as a revolving spit, grill, or metal rack. 4. Food that is prepared and served in a highly seasoned sauce. 5. A meat dish in which ground or finely chopped meat is prepared in a highly seasoned sauce and generally served in a bun.

The history of cooked meat is unclear. Probably, meat was first cooked when primitive man unintentionally dropped a piece of meat into the fire. No doubt, he was pleased with his discovery for meat has been cooked in this manner for centuries.

The origin of the word barbecue is just as unclear. Some authorities believe the term was first used by seventeenth-century French pirates who called it *de barbe a cue,* which meant cooking from "beard to tail." Others claim the word resulted from the Spanish word *barbacoa,* meaning a wooden rack or frame on which food was preserved by drying. The frame also was used for cooking meat over a roaring fire. Regardless of the place and date of origin, the meaning of barbecue has expanded considerably over the years.

The manner of supporting and turning meat over an open fire became more refined as civilization progressed. Primitive

Barbecuing at its best

←Juicy, tender Rotisseried Rolled Rib Roast cooks to perfection over glowing coals. Tangy basting sauce adds special flavor.

man in the Caribbean islands made portable racks of green wood, supported by four corner posts, on which to roast large chunks of meat, small animals, or fish.

Hunters learned to suspend small animals on a green stick, held by two forked sticks over a fire. Later, a spit was developed that could support the hindquarter of large animals. It was turned slowly during roasting by a kitchen boy. Smaller animals were roasted whole.

American colonists roasted meat in the fireplace by hanging the pieces of meat over the fire on a heavy string. The string was twisted to allow the meat to rotate during roasting. A short time later, a spit was installed in the fireplace with a drip pan under the meat to catch the drippings. Turning the spit was delegated to one of the family members. A faster method of cooking meat resulted when a three-sided metal roasting kitchen was invented. At the base of the metal enclosure was a drip pan with hinged lid. Thus, the meat could be basted periodically.

Today, barbecuing and barbecue equipment is more refined. Green wood racks and cooking coals have been replaced with metal grills and fireboxes, and mechanical rotisseries outdate hand-turned spits.

During the nineteenth century, an American barbecue referred to an outdoor gathering, generally political in nature. A barbecue included a feast of roasted meats in addition to political speeches and a band to liven the merriment. Little else accompanied the roasted meat other than homemade bread and plenty of beer, wine, and coffee. One measure of a man in that day was the amount of barbecue he could consume. Members of political parties competed with one another to see who could supply the largest amount of food to eat.

Preparation for the feast began many days in advance. On the appointed day, guests often traveled many miles to attend, arriving with ravenous appetites.

Fires were built in open pits over which the meat was roasted, suspended from wooden spits. The slaughtered animals might include sheep, beef, or pigs roasted whole, halved, or quartered. During the roasting, the meat was basted with hot, salted water. Once it was removed from the open fire, the meat was brushed with a mixture of lard and strong vinegar, seasoned with red and black pepper.

The barbecue was popular, perhaps, because of the number of people that could be served with relatively little inconvenience. Some writers referred to the barbecues of the day as events at which large numbers of sheep and cattle were roasted to feed thousands of guests.

Fire building

Wood and charcoal are the two fuels most often used for barbecue grilling. A wood fire takes longer to build and burn down to a bed of coals, satisfactory for cooking. Thus, if wood is used, the fire must be started about two hours in advance.

Dry, hard woods such as hickory, oak, maple, walnut, birch, ash, and pecan burn slowly giving long-burning coals and an even heat. A pleasant flavor is imparted to foods cooked over fruit woods. Soft woods are good for kindling since they light easily and burn quickly.

Start a wood fire with dry paper or other easily ignitable material. Add small, dry twigs until a good fire base is apparent. Then add larger pieces of dry, hard wood till the fire is the right size. The larger the wood pieces, the slower they burn.

Charcoal is the fuel most often purchased for barbecuing. To produce charcoal, large pieces of wood are slowly smoldered in an enclosed area such as a kiln. During this process, the wood is converted into odd-sized lumps that are porous, black, lightweight, and are called charcoal—composed primarily of carbon.

Charcoal is available in lumps or briquets. Lump charcoal is best suited for grilling fast-cooking foods such as small steaks or hamburgers. It is not as compact as briquets; thus it burns faster and less evenly. Charcoal briquets are made of ground charcoal mixed with a starch binder, then compressed into uniform blocks. Because of their uniformity, briquets burn more evenly and longer.

Briquets vary in the manner in which they burn due to different materials used to produce them. Some brands burn more rapidly than others, while some produce a more intense heat for a longer period of time. Some impart a special flavor to the food such as when hickory briquets are used. The flavor of hickory is pleasing to many people. Experimentation with various brands and types will determine the kind best suited for a particular situation.

Preparing the grill: Before building a fire in any type of grill, be certain to read the instruction booklet provided by the manufacturer. Different methods of fire building are recommended for different types of grills. When followed, they promote the life of the equipment as well as produce a more satisfactory heat.

Some manufacturers suggest lining the base of the firebox with *dry* pea gravel, coarse grit, or special insulating pellets. A bed of this material helps prevent burning out the bottom of the firebox. It also lets in air so that the heat is more evenly distributed. Dripping fats and juices are absorbed by the gravel, thus further protecting the firebox.

Another method for protecting the firebox is to line the box with heavy foil, shiny side up. The *dry* gravel or special pellets can be placed atop the foil. After grilling several times, the fat-soaked gravel and spattered foil can be removed easily and replaced. If desired, the gravel may be washed in hot water and spread out to *dry thoroughly,* then replaced in the firebox. (If gravel is not *thoroughly dried,* it may explode when heated.) Lining the firebox with heavy foil speeds up cooking since foil reflects heat from the coals up towards the food. As a result, food cooks faster.

Starting the fire: All fires require a draft to keep burning. Thus, just as with a wood fire, a charcoal fire must be built carefully if it is to burn evenly and for the length of time needed. When using a shallow fire bowl, a light breeze will generally provide enough draft to maintain the fire. Many of the deeper fire bowls have a draft control at the bottom of the fire bowl which is helpful in controlling the heat.

Pile the charcoal briquets in a pyramid in the firebox. Once the briquets begin to glow, the heat creates its own draft when built in this manner. The briquets may be lighted by placing scraps of paper and wood kindling in the center of the charcoal pyramid and igniting with a match. This, however, is more time-consuming and not always a successful method since briquets have a tendency to ignite slowly.

Use only as much charcoal as needed for the job at hand. Too large a fire not only produces too much heat but also it increases the cost of barbecuing.

A far more reliable method for starting a briquet fire is to use a liquid lighter. Sprinkle it on the charcoal slowly, giving it a chance to be absorbed by the briquets. Wait a few minutes; then light with a match in several places.

Never use kerosene or gasoline to start a fire as they are too dangerous. Also, kerosene gives food an unpleasant flavor.

Liquid starters are easily adapted to other fire building methods. Fill a metal container such as a two-pound coffee can with six briquets. Add liquid starter to cover briquets. Cover can tightly and let stand one hour or till briquets are thoroughly soaked. Place soaked briquets in the bottom of the firebox to start the fire. Build remaining fire with untreated briquets.

An electric starter is perhaps the fastest and cleanest method for starting a fire but an electrical outlet must be available. Place the heating element of the starter amid the briquets. Due to the intense heat from the starter, the briquets begin to burn within a few minutes. Some grills are equipped with a built-in starter.

Other commercial fire starters are available such as jellies, foams, cubes, sticks, and flakes. Canned heat is a convenient fire starter, particularly when all supplies must be transported. Put three or four tablespoons canned heat in a cup made of heavy foil. Place the cup in the firebox and heap the charcoal around and over it. Once the canned heat is ignited, the charcoal begins to burn.

Self-starting briquets are also available on the market. The briquets are packaged complete with starter. All the fire builder has to do is place the package in the firebox and light with a match. Although convenient for camping, this method is more expensive than when briquets and starter are purchased separately.

Once the fire is ignited, wait for the charcoal to begin burning. A few whitish-gray spots will appear in a few minutes. After 10 to 15 minutes, turn briquets which have a good covering of ash; this helps others to start. Allow about another 30 minutes for the coals to reach cooking temperature. They will appear ash-gray by day and glowing red after dark.

Arranging the coals: Using long-handled tongs, arrange the hot coals to cover the cooking area needed. For use of the full grill surface, spread the coals over all of the firebox. Keep coals in a smaller area for a single steak or a few chops. For kabobs, line up coals in parallel rows, spacing them between kabobs on the grill above. This allows even heat for cooking, yet reduces the possibility of flare-ups caused by fat dripping onto the hot coals.

If food is cooked on a spit with a reflector hood, pile coals a little higher than usual, slightly to the rear of the spit, and beyond the ends of the spitted meat. Use a drip pan under the meat. If using a spit in an open unit, arrange the coals in a ring around, and slightly larger than, the meat on the spit to insure even cooking.

Controlling the heat: Cooking temperature is important to producing barbecued food that is nicely browned, properly cooked, and juicy. A simple hand test can be used to indicate the hotness of the fire. Holding the hand over the fire, begin counting "one thousand one, one thousand two," and so on. The number of seconds the hand can comfortably be held over the fire is a guide to how hot the fire is. A "one thousand two" fire is relatively hot and perfect for the grilling of steaks, kabobs, and hamburgers. "One thousand three or four" is a moderate fire for roasts and other large pieces of meat. At "one thousand five or six" the fire is slow enough for cooking pork chops or spareribs.

Once the proper fire temperature is reached, it is necessary to maintain the fire at approximately the same temperature. If the fire becomes too hot, the heat must be reduced. To do so, lower the firebox, if it is adjustable, or raise the grill. If rotisserie cooking with the coals arranged in a ring beneath the spit, move the coals out, forming a larger ring.

If the fire appears to be weakening before the food is cooked, move the food closer to the coals by lowering the grill or raising the firebox. Or, tap the ashes off the coals with tongs as the ashes tend to insulate the burning coals. Open drafts to let more air through. If necessary to add more coals, warm extra briquets around the edge of the fire before placing them atop burning coals.

Occasionally, coals may flare up as a result of fat dripping onto the hot coals. Unless extinguished, these flare-ups will cause food to taste of burned fat. Keep a water pistol or clothes sprinkler filled with water handy. Use only enough water to extinguish flare-ups. If too much is used, coals will become soaked, thus reducing the temperature of the heat.

Cleaning the grill: After the food is cooked, smother the fire and save the coals to use again. If the barbecue unit has a hood, cover the unit to extinguish the fire. Or, remove the coals to a pail and cover tightly. Coals may be doused with water but must be spread out to *dry thoroughly* before being used again.

To simplify the cleanup, remove the grill from the firebox and wrap in wet paper toweling or wet newspapers. After the meal, the grill can be wiped clean. Scouring or abrasive-type pads may be needed for stubborn spots.

Equipment

Barbecue equipment may be as simple as an iron skillet full of charcoal or as elaborate as a custom-built unit with grill, ovens, and flues. Available on the market are open or covered grills and cookers designed to use, in various ways, heat or smoke from charcoal and wood to cook food. Many of the more elaborate units have warming ovens, self lighters, electric motor-driven rotisseries, storage drawers, and attached working surfaces.

Many of the grills can be raised or lowered to obtain the degree of heat desired. A few units have built-in thermometers in the hoods, useful if the unit is used as a smoke oven or covered cooker.

Various types of small grills are portable and suitable for cooking on the beach or at the campsite. Among these are the folding grills, which are small fireboxes topped with a grid and supported by folding legs. Bucket grills also transport easily. The fuel can be carried in the bucket, eliminating the need for another container. The top on some bucket grills can be used as a skillet for cooking.

Hibachis, Japanese firebowls, are another popular type of grill. Generally made of cast iron, they are also available in aluminum. Many hibachis have adjustable grids and all have draft doors. Available in many sizes, the very small hibachis are often used when entertaining to grill individual appetizers.

A brazier, no doubt the most common type of barbecue unit, is a shallow firebowl set on three or four legs and fitted with a wire grid. Some units have partial hoods. Many have a draft control at the bottom of the firebowl and adjustable grids. The more expensive braziers have detachable electric rotisserie units. Some are also equipped with wheels for easy moving.

Cooking kettles are very much like large Dutch ovens on legs. Made of heavy cast metal, many have wheels. They have adjustable dampers in both the lid and the bowl. The cost is somewhat more than many of the other types of barbecue units.

Gas grills, too, are fast gaining in popularity with the outdoor chef. Stationary or portable, they make year-round cooking possible. Some are equipped with ceramic briquets while others are designed with infrared units in the lid. Adjustable grills, rotisseries, variable heat settings, and side tables are found on many models. The lid may be raised for open broiling and closed

Deluxe braziers are equipped with a motorized spit, an adjustable grid and firebox for controlling fire temperature, and a half-hood to shield the fire from the wind. A warming oven with a heat indicator is an additional feature found on some units.

for smoking or baking. Quick fire-starting and reliable heat control are important features on the gas grill.

A smoke oven or cooker is an adaptation of a Chinese method of cooking. The chimney is located at one end of the firebox. The fire is built in the firebox and smoke travels up the chimney where food is suspended on a hook. Thus, it is cooked in the hot smoke rather than over the fire. A smoke oven may be permanent or portable, made of brick, ceramic, or metal.

Assorted barbecue tools and grill attachments are necessary in addition to the basic barbecue unit. The number and variety

A simple, portable-type brazier is ideal when barbecuing away from home. The small, shallow firebowl atop three short legs makes the unit convenient to use on a picnic table. Handles on the sides are useful in moving the grill when hot. The distance of the food from the fire is regulated by the screw-type grid adjustment at the side.

A barbecue oven on wheels—a cooking kettle makes possible many types of outdoor cooking. For open grilling, the lid is removed. Equipped with two grills, coals are placed on the bottom with food on the top. More expensive models feature dampers in both the lid and bowl with an ash-catcher underneath. Wheels plus handles on the bowl make the cooking kettle easy to move.

of extras, however, will depend greatly upon the enthusiasm and skill of the outdoor chef, as well as the frequency with which the family grills.

As a safety precaution, asbestos gloves or mitts and long-handled utensils should be used when working over a fire. One set of long-handled tongs should be used to handle coals and another set to handle the food. Different sized basting brushes as well as fireproof saucepans to hold sauces, marinades, or melted butter are convenient to have on hand. To prepare kabobs, skewers must be provided.

Broiler baskets simplify the cooking of food over a barbecue unit not equipped with an adjustable grid. The food, placed in a broiler basket, can be removed from the heat instantly by lifting the basket away from the fire. Thus, the distance between the food and the fire can be easily regulated and controlled.

Grill and meat thermometers are useful instruments for determining doneness as well as the hotness of the fire. A grill thermometer, placed on the grid or the spit, registers the temperature of the coals from the meat level. A meat thermometer indicates internal temperature and corresponding doneness without cutting into the meat. These tools help make outdoor barbecuing a much more reliable and controllable method of cooking.

Methods of cooking

Successful barbecuing is not limited to fire-building and equipment know-how. Although essential, these two aspects of outdoor cooking are merely preliminary to serving mouth-watering food prepared over an open fire. Much of the success of the barbecue is dependent upon the culinary skills of the chef.

Barbecue fans need not resign themselves to a monotonous menu when eating outdoors. Although special equipment is necessary in some cases, many barbecue units are adaptable to various cooking methods. Variety adds interest to outdoor cooking fun. Try roasting meat in a covered cooker; another time, roast meat on a spit. For kabobs, skewer meat cubes with vegetables and fruits before grilling.

Smoke cooking: The traditional method of smoke cooking is most easily achieved in a Chinese smoker where the food is hung in a chimney away from the fire. As the hot smoke rises up the chimney, the food is cooked and flavored with the smoke. Hickory, oak, maple, nut, and fruitwoods are most often used for the fire.

If a Chinese smoker is not available, a covered barbecue unit can be used. Allow the fire to burn until a smokeless heat is produced. Arrange the coals away from where the food is placed. Sprinkle the coals with *damp* wood chips or *damp* sawdust to produce a dense smoke. Lower the hood. Add *dampened* wood chips periodically to maintain a constant smoke.

To prepare wood chips, soak chips in water for 10 to 20 minutes before using. Remove any chips that catch fire and soak again before returning them to the fire. Use dampers in the unit to control the temperature of the fire.

Kowloon Duckling

    1 4- to 5-pound ready-to-cook
        duckling
    1 bunch green onions (6 to 8
        onions), cut up
    6 sprigs parsley
    3 cloves garlic, quartered
    ½ cup soy sauce
    ¼ cup honey

Clean duckling; stuff with onion, parsley, and garlic. Skewer neck and body cavities closed; tie securely with cord. Insert hook from smoker through tail of duckling and over skewer that closes the body cavity. Blend together soy sauce and honey; heat. For a brown glaze, brush duckling with soy mixture every 5 minutes for 1 hour *before* hanging in smoke oven.

Then hang duckling in 275° to 300° Chinese smoke oven which uses wood as fuel—split logs of fruitwood, oak, or hickory. Smoke duckling about 3½ hours, or until bird is tender and a deep golden brown color.

To carve: Remove wings, cut off leg and second joint. Make lengthwise cuts on both sides of breast bone, cutting down to the bone. Place knife in first cut; carve along breastbone to free the slices. Makes 4 servings.

Hickory Smoked Turkey

> 1 14- to 16-pound turkey
> 1 tablespoon salt
> Butter or margarine, melted

Rub inside of turkey with salt. Skewer neck skin to back. Insert spit; anchor turkey with holding forks. Check balance. With cord tie wings of turkey flat against body. With another piece of cord, tie legs of turkey to tail. Attach spitted bird to rotisserie.

Arrange *medium-slow* coals at back and sides of firebox and a foil drip pan under bird. Using basting brush, brush bird with melted butter or margarine. Lower hood of barbecue unit and start rotisserie. Sprinkle *dampened* hickory chips over coals every 20 to 30 minutes; brush bird with additional melted butter or margarine occasionally. Roast 5 to 5½ hours. Allow ½ to ¾ pound per serving.

Smoked Fish with Lemon

> 6 fish steaks or fillets, ¾
>   to 1 inch thick
> Salt and pepper
> 2 or 3 lemons, *thinly* sliced
> ½ cup butter or margarine, melted
> 1 or 2 cloves garlic, minced

Sprinkle fish generously with salt and pepper. Arrange *half* of the lemon slices in bottom of a foil baking pan; arrange the fish over lemon slices in single layer. Place remaining lemon slices atop and around sides. Combine melted butter and garlic; pour over fish. Sprinkle *dampened* hickory chips over *slow* coals. Place baking dish on heavy foil atop grill.

Close smoker hood; cook slowly, about 1 hour, turning once. Baste fish frequently with butter mixture. Serve with the cooked lemon slices and butter mixture. Makes 6 servings.

Eye-catching Hickory Smoked Turkey reigns supreme at the barbecue. The bird cooks over smoking wood chips. Skewered tomatoes and summer squash complete the entrée.

Cooking kabobs: Innumerable food combinations make kabobs a versatile choice for barbecuing. A blending of flavors, colors, and textures is possible when a variety of meats, vegetables, and fruits are skewered together for grilling.

Quick-cooking meats or those which can be served slightly rare are best to use. If long cooking is required, the small cubes of meat become dry. Chunks of tender beef, lamb, shrimp, lobster, fully cooked ham, franks, and canned meat are ideal. Less tender cuts of meat are suitable if a tenderizer or marinade is used.

Vegetables that can be eaten slightly crisp make good kabob partners. Thus, cucumber slices, green pepper squares, onion wedges, and mushroom caps are perfect mates. Longer cooking vegetables such as small new potatoes, carrots, baby patty pan squashes, and tiny eggplants are best if partially cooked before skewering.

To thread skewers, pierce each kabob through center to balance. Let only those foods that cook in the same amount of time share the same skewer. Thread longer cooking foods on separate skewers and place on the fire earlier. Allow a little space between foods for more even cooking. Wedge fragile foods such as pineapple chunks or tomato wedges between firmer foods to prevent losing them in the fire. Or, use double skewers or twisted skewers to hold food more securely.

Cook kabobs over *hot* coals that are arranged in parallel rows in the firebox. Rest skewers on grill between rows of coals. Thus, drippings from kabobs are less likely to fall on burning coals, reducing the possibility of flare-ups.

During grilling, baste kabobs with melted butter or a marinade to keep them moist. Brush sweet barbecue sauces on toward the end; otherwise kabobs get too dark.

Kabobs readily lend themselves to spur-of-the-moment cooking. Therefore, late-arriving guests needn't be served cold food. Let each person skewer his favorite foods, creating his own tasty combo.

For other kabob fare, skewer chunks of French bread and toast over the grill. Thread marshmallows, fruits, or cake cubes on skewers for dessert. Or, serve tiny kabobs as appetizers grilled over a hibachi.

Meatball Barbecue

   1 beaten egg
 ¼ cup milk
 ½ cup quick-cooking rolled oats
   1 teaspoon Worcestershire sauce
 ½ teaspoon salt
 ¼ teaspoon dry mustard
1½ pounds ground beef
  20 large pimiento-stuffed green
       olives
       Bottled barbecue sauce

Combine first 6 ingredients and dash pepper. Add beef; mix well. Shape meat around olives, forming 20 meatballs. Thread balls on skewers pushing skewer through olive. Brush with barbecue sauce. Grill over *hot* coals 8 minutes. Turn; brush again with barbecue sauce. Grill 4 minutes longer. Makes 5 or 6 servings.

Lamb Kabobs

In mixing bowl, combine 1 cup rosé wine; ½ cup orange juice; ½ cup finely chopped onion; ¼ cup chili sauce; ¼ cup salad oil; 1 clove garlic, minced; 1 tablespoon brown sugar; 1 teaspoon salt; 1 teaspoon dried oregano leaves, crushed; and ¼ teaspoon pepper. Place 2 pounds boneless lamb, cut in 2-inch cubes, in a bowl. Pour wine mixture over lamb. Cover; marinate lamb for 2 hours at room temperature or overnight in refrigerator. Drain lamb, reserving marinade.

In small saucepan, pour boiling water over 12 fresh whole mushrooms (5-ounce carton); let mushrooms stand for 2 minutes. Drain. Cut 2 green peppers into 1½-inch squares. Thread lamb cubes, green pepper squares, and mushrooms alternately on skewers. Broil 4 to 6 inches from heat for 25 to 30 minutes, turning skewers frequently and brushing with reserved marinade. Makes 6 servings.

Cake Kabobs

Cut pound or angel cake in 1½-inch cubes. Spear each on fork; dip cake cubes in melted currant jelly or in sweetened condensed milk. Then roll in flaked coconut to cover. String cubes on skewers and toast over *very hot* coals, turning often, till kabobs are golden.

Appetizer Skewer Dogs

       1 beaten egg
       2 tablespoons milk
       1 cup soft bread crumbs (about
             1½ slices)
       2 tablespoons chopped onion
       ½ teaspoon salt
       1 pound ground beef
     16 cocktail sausages
     16 dill pickle slices
       1 cup catsup
       ¼ cup butter or margarine
       ¼ cup dark corn syrup
       2 tablespoons vinegar

Combine first 5 ingredients and dash pepper. Add beef; mix thoroughly. Chill. Form into 16 meatballs. Thread cocktail sausages, pickle slices, and meatballs alternately on skewers. Grill kabobs over *medium* coals about 18 minutes, turning once or twice.

Meanwhile, combine catsup, butter, corn syrup, and vinegar in saucepan. Simmer while kabobs cook. Brush sauce on kabobs just before removing from heat. Makes 16 appetizers.

Barbecued Vegetables

Scrub baking potatoes, yams, turnips, and tomatoes. Leave all whole in jackets. String each kind of vegetable on its own skewer. Rotate on motorized skewers over *hot* coals that are lined up in rows between skewers.

Allow 45 to 60 minutes for potatoes and 30 minutes for turnips. Put tomatoes on last. If done before meat, wrap vegetables in foil and keep warm away from coals on grill.

Powwow Sundae

       ¼ pound large marshmallows
       1 cup chocolate syrup
           Vanilla ice cream

String marshmallows on skewers. Toast over coals till melted inside and well-browned on outside. (If desired, let marshmallows blaze slightly for crusty edges.) Slip hot marshmallows off skewers into serving bowl of chocolate syrup. Stir just to marble, then ladle over scoops of ice cream. Makes 1½ cups sauce.

Lace steak strips on skewers for hibachi-grilled Island Teriyaki. Marinade and water chestnuts add an oriental flavor.

Island Teriyaki

       1½ pounds top sirloin steak
       ½ cup soy sauce
       ¼ cup brown sugar
       2 tablespoons olive oil
       1 tablespoon grated gingerroot
           or 1 teaspoon ground ginger
       2 cloves garlic, minced
           Canned water chestnuts

Cut meat in strips ¼ inch thick and 1 inch wide. Mix soy, next 4 ingredients, and ¼ teaspoon pepper. Add meat; stir to coat. Let stand 2 hours at room temperature. Skewer meat accordion-style; add water chestnuts at ends. Broil over *hot* coals 10 to 12 minutes; turn often. Baste with marinade. Serves 4 or 5.

Open grilling: Beef cuts tender enough for broiling are excellent choices for the outdoor barbecue. Less tender beef steaks such as bottom round, blade, chuck, and flank require marinating or tenderizing before grilling. Pork favorites for the grill include chops, steaks, Canadian-style bacon, ribs, fully cooked ham slice, smoked sausage links, and fully cooked specialty sausages. Lamb chops are also popular choices. In addition, chicken, fish, seafood, ground beef, and ground lamb are perfect barbecue fare prepared over an open fire. Regardless of the meat selected, it should be cut at least 1 inch thick for grilling.

The fire is ready when the coals appear ash-gray and the temperature is right according to the hand test (see pp. 147-148). With long-handled tongs, arrange coals to cover an area slightly larger than the food on the grill. Allow a little space between coals to insure even heat.

Reduce flare-ups by trimming excess fat from outer edges of steaks, chops, and ham slices. If drippings flare up during grilling, sprinkle coals lightly with water to quench the blaze.

Slash fat edges (but not into meat) before grilling to keep meat flat as it cooks. Or, cook in a broiler basket to keep it from cupping. Using a broiler basket is good barbecue technique when grilling fish, chicken pieces, shrimp, or other meats which are difficult to turn on the grill.

Steaks are ready to turn when little bubbles appear on the top surface of the meat. Then flip with long-handled tongs and pancake turner. Avoid piercing meat with a fork as flavorful juices are lost.

Grilling time depends upon the thickness of the meat, the temperature of the fire, and the degree of doneness desired. However, avoid turning meat more than once, allowing a few more minutes on the first side than the second. (The second side cooks faster since it has been heated.) Grilling time for chicken is reduced if cooked bone side down first. The bone helps transmit the heat through the meat, speeding up cooking time.

Season meat with salt and pepper after browning. Season second side after removing it from the grill. If done before cooking, salt draws out important juices.

Fresh herb flavor can be added to grilling meats by tossing fresh herbs on coals near the end of the cooking period. Or, add smoky wood flavor to meat by sprinkling *dampened* wood chips over coals.

Brush marinades or sauces on meat after it begins cooking. They help keep meat moist as well as add flavor. If a tomato or sweet barbecue sauce is used, wait till last 15 minutes of cooking before basting; otherwise, meat becomes too dark.

Butterfly Leg of Lamb

      1   5- to 6-pound leg of lamb
    ½   cup lemon juice
    ½   cup salad oil
    ¼   cup grated onion
      1   or 2 cloves garlic, minced
      1   teaspoon salt
      1   teaspoon *fines herbes*
    ½   teaspoon pepper
    ½   teaspoon dried thyme leaves,
          crushed

Have meatman bone leg of lamb and slit lengthwise to spread flat like a thick steak. In shallow baking pan blend remaining ingredients. Place meat in marinade. Let stand one hour at room temperature *or* overnight in refrigerator; turn meat occasionally.

Remove meat; reserve marinade. Insert 2 long skewers through meat at right angles making an X *or* place in wire broiler basket for easy turning and to keep meat from "curling."

Roast over *medium* coals 1½ to 2 hours, turning every 15 minutes till medium or well done. Baste frequently with reserved marinade. Remove skewers; cut across grain into thin slices. Makes 8 servings.

Smoked Linkburgers

Combine 1 pound ground beef, 1 tablespoon brown sugar, 1 tablespoon finely chopped onion, 1 tablespoon lemon juice, ½ teaspoon salt, and dash pepper; mix thoroughly. Divide meat mixture into 8 portions. Using one 12-ounce package (8) smoked sausage links, mold ground meat around each link. Grill over *medium* coals for 18 to 20 minutes, turning kabobs frequently. Makes 8 servings.

Grilled Turkey Pieces

    1 6- to 7-pound ready-to-cook
        turkey
    ¼ cup salad oil
    ¼ cup soy sauce
    1 tablespoon honey
    1 teaspoon ground ginger
    1 teaspoon dry mustard
    1 clove garlic, minced

Cut turkey as follows: 2 wings, 2 drumsticks, 2 thighs, 4 breast pieces, and 2 back pieces. Combine remaining ingredients for marinade. Place turkey in marinade 2 hours at room temperature *or* overnight in refrigerator. Place drumsticks, thighs, and breast pieces on grill 6 to 8 inches above *medium-hot* coals. (Add wings and back 30 minutes later.) Broil, turning occasionally, for 1 hour. Baste with marinade; broil 30 minutes more. Turkey is done when thigh muscle is fork-tender. Makes 10 to 12 servings.

Shrimp-Out

    1 pound fresh or frozen shrimp
        in shells
    1 slightly beaten egg
    ½ cup crushed saltine crackers
    ⅓ cup salad oil

Peel and clean shrimp. Dip each shrimp in egg, then in crumbs. Let stand in oil 1 minute; lightly drain on paper toweling. Cook over *hot* coals 5 to 8 minutes or till browned. Serve with hot sauce, if desired. To prevent shrimp from falling through grill, cover grid with screen wire or cake rack, *or* cook in broiler basket. Makes 3 or 4 servings.

Barbecued Bologna Burgers

Cut large, chunk bologna into slices ½ inch thick. Score bologna slices lightly on both sides; brush with melted butter. Grill over *hot* coals till browned. Serve on hamburger buns, split and toasted. Add assorted toppings—chopped onion; pickle relish; sour cream with minced onion and green pepper; crumbled blue cheese; whipped cream cheese flavored with bacon and horseradish; whipped cream cheese flavored with Roquefort; or other packaged dip.

Zesty Luncheon Barbecue

    1 small onion, chopped (½ cup)
    2 tablespoons butter or margarine
    1 cup catsup
    ¼ cup brown sugar
    3 tablespoons vinegar
    1 tablespoon Worcestershire sauce
    1 tablespoon prepared mustard
    2 12-ounce cans luncheon meat
        Sliced sourdough or French bread

In small skillet cook onion in butter till tender but not brown. Stir in ⅓ cup water, catsup, and next 4 ingredients; mix well. Cut meat into 12 slices. Place meat on grill; brush with sauce. Grill over *medium-hot* coals 5 to 6 minutes per side, brushing occasionally with sauce. Serve on bread as closed or open-face sandwiches. Makes 6 servings.

Outdoor Burgers

    ¼ cup chopped onion
    2 tablespoons finely chopped
        green pepper (optional)
    3 tablespoons catsup
    1 tablespoon prepared horseradish
    1 teaspoon salt
    2 teaspoons prepared mustard
    1 pound ground beef

Combine first 6 ingredients and dash pepper. Add beef; mix well. Shape into 4 patties ½ inch thick. Broil over *hot* coals 5 minutes. Turn; broil 3 minutes more. Makes 4 servings.

Rotisserie cooking: Beef rib roasts (rolled or standing), rolled rump roasts (prime quality), rolled fresh pork roasts, spareribs, Canadian-style bacon, boned and rolled lamb roasts, lamb racks, chicken, turkey, and duckling are excellent choices for spit-cooking. Since the meat bastes itself as it rotates, a fair amount of fat is necessary to insure juicy meat.

Much of the success of rotisserie cooking depends upon mounting the meat correctly on the spit. For poultry, truss with heavy string or skewers to prevent wings and legs from flopping. Large rolled roasts should be tied at intervals. To mount

on spit, slip one of the holding forks onto the spit rod. Push the rod through the center of the meat, inserting the tines of holding fork firmly into the meat. Push in second holding fork; fasten. Test the balance by cradling the ends of the rod in upturned hands and rotating meat. If it twirls evenly, it balances. If not, remount meat and test balance again; or, add metal weights (available on some spits) to balance.

The most reliable guide to meat doneness is a meat thermometer. When inserting, make certain bulb doesn't touch bone, fat, or metal spit. For poultry, insert the thermometer in the thickest part of the thigh muscle. For roasts, insert at an angle or parallel to spit. Watch that thermometer clears bottom of grill.

Arrangement of the hot coals depends upon the type of barbecue unit used (see p. 149). To reduce flare-ups and cleanup, place a drip pan made from heavy duty foil under meat to catch drippings. After cooking, the drip pan can be discarded.

Just as with kabobs and open grilling, sauces are often used for basting. Delay brushing with tomato or very sweet barbecue sauces till the last 30 minutes of cooking; otherwise, the meat gets too dark.

Lamb Racks with Herb Jackets

Select three 7-rib racks of lamb; have meatman saw chine bone between chops for easier carving. Balance on spit; insert meat thermometer, not touching spit, fat, or bone. Using ring of *hot* coals around meat and drip pan underneath, let meat rotate till thermometer reads 175°— about 1½ hours.

Finely crush ½ cup packaged herb-seasoned stuffing croutons. Toss with 2 tablespoons snipped parsley. Sprinkle seasoned crouton mixture over fat side of lamb often during last 15 minutes of cooking, until even "jacket" is formed. Makes 9 servings.

Dinner-on-a-spit

←Watch outdoor fans savor the aroma of Lamb Racks with Herb Jackets. Squash and eggplant kabobs complete the meal.

Rotisserie Round

> 1 3-pound eye of beef round roast
> Instant unseasoned meat tenderizer
> 1 cup catsup
> 1 cup water
> ⅓ cup Worcestershire sauce
> 1 teaspoon salt
> 1 teaspoon chili powder
> 1 small clove garlic, minced

Sprinkle all sides of meat with tenderizer, using ½ teaspoon per pound. *Do not use additional salt.* To insure penetration, pierce meat deeply at ½-inch intervals with long-tined fork. Meanwhile, combine remaining ingredients; simmer slowly for 30 minutes.

Center meat on spit and tie securely with cord. Roast over *medium-low* coals on motorized spit about 1½ hours, or to desired doneness, basting frequently with the sauce.

Meat thermometer will read 140° for rare, 160° for medium, or 170° for well done. To serve, slice steak on bias, across grain; pass remaining sauce. Makes 8 servings.

Orange-Pork Curry

> 1 4- to 5-pound pork loin roast*
> 1 orange, unpeeled and cut in thin wedges
> 1 cup syrup from canned fruit
> ½ cup brown sugar
> ¼ cup vinegar
> 1 tablespoon curry powder
> 2 tablespoons salad oil
> 2 tablespoons soy sauce

*Have meatman loosen backbone from ribs but leave attached. Cut to within 1 inch of backbone in 1-inch chops. In each slit, insert orange wedge, peel side out. Insert skewer lengthwise near edge through chops and fruit. Tie roast with cord, end to end, and in 2 or 3 places between. Insert rotisserie spit; balance roast, securing with holding forks. Season meat with salt and pepper.

Roast on rotisserie, with hood down, over *medium* coals for 2 to 2½ hours, or till done. Meanwhile, combine remaining ingredients for sauce. Raise hood during last 30 minutes and brush meat with sauce. Makes 8 servings.

Ribs Dee-Lish

    3 to 4 pounds meaty spareribs,
        sawed in lengthwise strips 4
        to 5 inches wide
    ½ cup apricot nectar
    ½ cup drained, crushed pineapple
    ½ cup catsup
    2 teaspoons lemon juice

Lace ribs on spit accordion-style; secure with holding forks. Arrange hot coals at back of firebox; place drip pan in front, under ribs, Rotate over *medium-low* coals, with hood down, for 1 to 1¼ hours, or till done. Combine remaining ingredients, ½ teaspoon salt, and dash pepper. During last 15 minutes, brush ribs often with sauce. Makes 3 or 4 servings.

Gourmet Tenderloin on a Spit

Flavored with blue cheese—

Trim fat from surface of 2 to 2½ pounds center cut beef tenderloin. Make a slanting cut, 2 inches deep, full length of meat with sharp knife held at a 45-degree angle. Make second cut on opposite side of tenderloin.

Crumble 4 ounces blue cheese (1 cup). Blend with 1 tablespoon brandy. Spread in openings formed by cuts. Skewer closed with short skewers. Tie at ends and in middle. Balance on spit; rotate over *hot* coals 1¼ to 1½ hours for medium rare. Serves 6 to 8.

Rotisseried Rolled Rib Roast

Select a 5- to 6-pound rolled rib roast. Have meatman tie roast at 1-inch intervals with heavy cord. (If lean, have outside covered with a thin layer of fat, then trussed securely.) Insert spit; adjust holding forks. Balance; insert meat thermometer so tip is in center but not touching fat or spit.

Arrange hot coals at back of firebox, and drip pan in front under roast. Rotate over *hot* coals about 2 to 2½ hours for medium rare. Thermometer will register 140° for rare, 160° for medium, and 170° for well-done. Heat ½ cup extra-hot catsup with ½ cup butter till blended. Brush on meat last 15 to 20 minutes. Allow 2 or 3 servings per pound.

Barbecued accompaniments: In addition to barbecuing meats, outdoor grilling provides the opportunity for adding a smoky flavor to vegetables, breads, desserts, and beverages. Thus, a complete meal cooked over the grill is possible.

Many vegetables adapt readily to outdoor cooking. Use skewers to grill vegetable kabobs or thread longer-cooking vegetables on spit and rotate over coals. Corn roasts to perfection in its own husks, a welcome addition to any barbecue. Likewise, the tantalizing aroma of baked beans cooked slowly over the fire is a must for a real western-style barbecue. Or, try heating canned or frozen vegetables. Season vegetables and wrap tightly in foil. Turn occasionally to distribute heat. Allow more time for the frozen ones.

Toast bread over the open grill or wrap buttered slices in foil and heat. Brown-and-serve rolls cook evenly when rotated on the spit and brushed with butter.

Foil dinners are the answer when equipment is limited. Select meat, vegetables, and/or fruits which are compatible in flavor. Cut longer-cooking foods in smaller pieces so all foods cook in the same amount of time. Wrap in foil, allowing space for expansion of steam. Cook over coals and serve as a compete meal-in-one.

Corned Beef and Cabbage Bundles

    1 12-ounce can corned beef
    1 medium head cabbage, shredded
        (8 cups)
    4 medium carrots, shredded
        (2 cups)
    ½ envelope (¼ cup) dry onion
        soup mix
    2 tablespoons butter or margarine

Slice corned beef into fourths. In bowl toss together cabbage, carrot, and soup mix. Divide into 4 portions. Tear off four 12-inch squares of heavy foil. Place vegetable portions in center of foil squares. Dot each with ½ tablespoon butter. Top each with corned beef slice. Draw up corners of foil to center; twist securely allowing room for expansion of steam. Grill over *medium* coals about 10 minutes, or till vegetables are tender. Makes 4 servings.

Roasted Corn

Remove husks from fresh corn. Remove silk with a stiff brush. Place each ear on a piece of foil. Spread corn liberally with softened butter and sprinkle with salt and pepper. Wrap in foil (fold or twist around ends, but don't seal seam). Roast over *hot* coals 15 to 20 minutes or till tender, turning frequently. Pass extra butter, salt, and pepper.

Indian-Style Corn on the Cob

Turn back corn husks; strip off silk. (If desired, wrap partially cooked bacon slice spiral-fashion around each ear.) Lay husks back in position. Roast over *hot* coals, turning frequently, 15 to 20 minutes, or till husks are dry and browned. (Longer roasting gives sweeter, more caramelized corn.) Pass *Whipped Anise Butter:* Pour 1 teaspoon boiling water over 1 teaspoon anise seed; let stand 30 minutes. Cream ½ cup butter or margarine, softened, till light and fluffy; stir in anise with liquid.

Spitted Vegetables

String small crookneck and/or patty pan squash on spit; secure with long holding fork. Brush with melted butter. Spin over *hot* coals 45 minutes or till done; baste occasionally.

Peel eggplant and cut in 2-inch chunks. String on spit; spin over *hot* coals 30 minutes or till tender, basting occasionally with melted butter. To keep vegetables hot after cooking, leave on spit and wrap loosely in foil; move to side of grill until serving time.

Hobo Rice

- 1½ cups water
- ½ teaspoon salt
- 1⅓ cups uncooked packaged precooked rice

Combine water and salt in a 1-pound size coffee can. Heat to boiling over *hot* coals. *Remove from heat;* add uncooked rice. Stir just to moisten. Cover tightly with metal lid or foil. Remove from grill, *away from heat;* let stand at least 13 minutes. Makes 3 cups.

Grilled Vegetables in Foil

- ½ pound fresh green beans, cut in 1-inch pieces
- 2 tomatoes, sliced
- ¼ cup chopped onion
- ¼ cup butter or margarine, softened
- 1 tablespoon brown sugar
- 1 teaspoon salt
- 2 teaspoons prepared mustard
- 1 teaspoon prepared horseradish
  Dash pepper

Cook green beans in a little boiling water for 10 minutes; drain. Place drained beans on a large, double-thick square of foil. Top with tomato slices. Combine chopped onion, butter, brown sugar, salt, mustard, horseradish, and pepper; beat till fluffy. Dot onion-butter mixture over green beans and tomatoes. Wrap vegetables tightly in foil, sealing edges. Cook vegetables 30 to 35 minutes over *medium-hot* coals. Makes 4 or 5 servings.

Barbecue Breads

Grilled Garlic Slices: Melt a little butter or margarine in shallow pan over grill; add garlic powder *or* minced garlic to taste. Toast thick slices of French bread on grill. Dip toasted slices into garlic butter. Serve hot.

Rolls on a Spit: Thread brown-and-serve rolls on rotisserie spit. Brush with melted butter; rotate over coals 10 to 15 minutes.

Scallion-Buttered Hard Rolls: Blend ½ cup butter or margarine, softened; 1 tablespoon finely chopped scallions; 1 tablespoon finely snipped parsley; and ¼ to ½ teaspoon dried rosemary leaves, crushed. Halve 6 hard rolls; spread with butter mixture. Wrap in foil; heat on grill 10 minutes or till hot.

Easy Onion Bread: Combine 2 teaspoons instant minced onion with 1 tablespoon water; let stand 5 minutes. Combine with ½ cup butter or margarine, softened, and 2 tablespoons snipped parsley. Mix well. Using 1 unsliced loaf French bread (about 18 inches long), slash bread on the bias in 1-inch slices, *cutting to but not through* bottom crust. Spread onion-butter generously on one side of each slice. Wrap loaf in foil. Heat on grill 20 to 30 minutes or till hot; turn occasionally. Serve hot.

BARBERRY *(bär' ber' ē)*—A prickly shrub that yields oblong dark red berries.

Pungently-tart jam, jelly, preserves, syrup, and candied barberries are made from the ripe berries. Barberry jam, jelly, or preserves are delicious as a meat accompaniment. (See also *Berry*.)

BAR COOKIE—Any variety and flavor of cookie that is cut in oblongs, squares, or diamonds after being baked. Bar cookies may contain fruits, nuts, cereal flakes, coconut, or they may consist of two layers with filling between.

This type of cookie is made with a stiff dough that is spread or pressed evenly into a square or oblong baking pan. After baking and cooling slightly, the cookies are cut into the desired shape.

Watch overbaking since it produces a dry, crumbly bar. Fudgy-type bars are done when the crust is dull and a slight imprint remains after touching with finger. Cake-like bars should be baked until a wooden pick inserted in the center of the pan comes out clean. (See also *Cookie*.)

Chocolate Diamonds

A chewy cookie full of semisweet chocolate pieces and nuts. Great for after-school snacks—

⅓ cup shortening
1 cup brown sugar
1 teaspoon vanilla
1 egg
1 cup sifted all-purpose flour
¼ teaspoon baking soda
¼ teaspoon salt
½ to 1 cup semisweet chocolate
    pieces
½ cup chopped walnuts

In mixing bowl thoroughly cream shortening, brown sugar, and vanilla. Add egg and beat well. Sift together the sifted flour, baking soda, and salt; add to creamed mixture, mixing well. Stir in semisweet chocolate pieces and chopped walnuts. Spread evenly in greased 11x7x1½-inch baking pan.

Bake at 350° for 20 to 25 minutes. Cool slightly; cut in diamond shapes or bars while warm. Makes about 2 dozen cookies.

A favorite with all ages, moist and chewy Fudge Brownies are bar cookies at their best (See *Brownie* for recipe). Dress up the brownies with a pretty pink frosting and marshmallow cuts.

Layer Bar Cookies

½ cup butter or margarine
1 cup graham-cracker crumbs
1 6-ounce package (1 cup)
    semisweet chocolate pieces
1 6-ounce package (1 cup)
    butterscotch pieces
1⅓ cups flaked coconut
½ cup chopped walnuts
1 15-ounce can sweetened
    condensed milk

Melt butter or margarine in 13x9x2-inch baking pan. Sprinkle crumbs evenly over butter. Layer with chocolate and butterscotch pieces, flaked coconut, and walnuts. Pour sweetened condensed milk over all. Bake at 350° for 30 minutes. Cool. Cut in bars.

BAR-LE-DUC *(bar luh dook)*—A sweet fruit spread manufactured in Bar-le-Duc, France, and used like a jelly or jam.

Although only red and white currants were originally used, today Bar-le-Duc is made also with black currants, raspberries, strawberries, and gooseberries. Each berry is seeded individually by piercing it with a special needlelike instrument so carefully that the seed is removed without destroying the round shape of the berry. The whole berries are then suspended in a crystal-clear jelly.

A favorite way of serving Bar-le-Duc is with a rich cream cheese and sweet crackers as a dessert or use it in Cumberland Sauce and serve with baked ham.

BARLEY—A hardy cereal grass which, because of its short growing season, can be grown in climates that range from subtropical to arctic. Both winter and spring varieties of this cereal are cultivated.

Barley was one of the earliest food plants known to man. It is mentioned in the Bible as one of the foods destroyed during the plagues of Egypt. It was cultivated by the ancient Greeks, Romans, and early English, and there is record of lake dwellers in present day Switzerland cultivating the cereal about 3,000 years ago. Barley made its appearance in America in the early part of the seventeenth century.

Because barley contains very little of the proteins necessary to hold the bread structure, barley flour cannot be used to make a high-rising loaf of bread. A combination of wheat and barley flour, however, will yield an acceptable though very compact loaf of bread.

The milled grain, husked and polished, is called pearl barley. In this country, the nut-flavored pearl barley is used primarily in Scotch broth or other soups and in simple hearty stews. Quick-cooking barley, which has been processed to reduce the cooking time, is a flavorful addition to casseroles or quick-cooking main dishes.

Although barley is an important food in India, Tibet, and Japan, elsewhere great quantities are grown for industrial production of barley malt. (See also *Grain.*)

BARLEY MALT—Malted barley used in preparing a fermentation mash for beer, Scotch whiskey, and vinegar.

Special types of barley grown and carefully ripened for malting are steeped in water and allowed to sprout, then heat-dried to stop germination. After being cured and ground, the malt is ready to use.

Since the yeasts used in brewing and distilling will work only on sugar, the malting process is necessary to convert the starch in unmalted grain to sugar.

Fine malted barley is one of the ingredients added to milk to make the beverage, malted milk. (See also *Malt.*)

BARLEY SUGAR—A clear candy originally made with barley water, sugar, and flavoring. The candy, often cut in long, thin, yellow transparent strips is now usually made without barley water. Old-fashioned molded barley sugar animals, traditional Christmas stocking stuffers, were variously flavored and colored.

BARLEY WATER—A beverage made by boiling a small quantity of pearl barley in a large quantity of water, then straining out the grain. In Victorian times most English households served barley water as a regular beverage. Since it is easily digested and provides a small amount of protein, barley water was also used as a food for infants and invalids.

BARON OF BEEF—A huge and impressive roast of beef consisting of the two sirloins joined at the backbone. This cut is too large to roast in any but the largest of institutional ovens or over an open fire. Baron of beef is somewhat freely used on restaurant menus to describe the roasted full rib or round of beef. The word baron is also applied to the two hind legs and saddle of any animal (particularly lamb) roasted as a whole. (See also *Beef*.)

BARQUETTE *(bär ket')*—A tiny oval-shaped pastry shell. The word barquette means "small boat" and describes the shape of these pastry shells. Barquettes may be filled with fruit and served as a dessert or filled with creamed lobster, mussels, shrimp, oysters, or other savory and served as an hors d'oeurve.

BARTLETT PEAR—A juicy, bell-shaped, all-purpose, summer pear. When ripe, this pear is creamy yellow with a slight red blush. The flesh is creamy white, fine grained, and highly aromatic.

This pear was found growing wild in England by an English school teacher in 1770. A nurseryman named Williams first distributed this pear and in Europe, it is still known as the Williams pear.

In 1798, the Williams pear was brought to the United States and planted in a Massachusetts orchard. The pear was then forgotten until 1817 when Enoch Bartlett bought the orchard. Not knowing its real name, Bartlett sold some of these trees under his own name. This name was later accepted in the United States and this variety of pear has been known as the Bartlett pear ever since.

Production of the Bartlett pear is largely confined to temperate zones. It is the leading pear sold in the United States with California, Oregon, and Washington as the major producers.

Fresh Bartlett pears are available from July to October. When selecting fresh Bartletts look for clean, uninjured fruit that is firm but not hard. Pears that are still green will ripen after purchase if left at room temperature. Fruit that is soft, shriveled, wilted, bruised, or noticeably misshapen should not be purchased.

Although the season for the fresh Bartlett pear is short, this variety is canned for use all year round. It is favored for canning because the canned Bartlett pear retains so much of the flavor, texture, and color of the fresh fruit.

Fresh Bartlett pears are excellent for eating raw but may lose their shape when poached or baked. A fresh Bartlett pear and a wedge of mild cheese make an easy and tasty summer dessert.

Canned Bartletts are excellent served chilled for dessert or used in salads, sauces, preserves, fruit compotes, coffee cakes, pastries, and as a meat accompaniment. (See also *Pear*.)

BASIL *(baz' uhl)*—Any of five or six varieties of an annual herb which belongs to the mint family. These varieties differ in height and taste and range in color from green to purple. Some varieties are grown for their ornamental foliage. This herb will grow in most climates.

A native of India and Iran, basil is now cultivated throughout the world. The Greeks liked this herb so well that they gave it the name basil—"King of the Herbs." Hindus consider basil sacred and plant it around their homes and temples to insure happiness. Following an old Italian custom, a suitor might wear a sprig of basil in his hair to publicly indicate his matrimonial intentions.

Sweet basil adds a pleasant spicy aroma and taste to meats, vegetables, salads, soups, Italian dishes, and any tomato dish.

The principal variety of basil grown is sweet basil. This variety has a pleasant spicy aroma and taste and is the type of basil most frequently used in cooking. The less well known purple basil lends an interesting color note as well as a distinctive flavor to foods.

The basil leaves and tender stems are used either fresh or dried. When bruised, the leaves have a fragrance reminiscent of cloves. Dried basil leaves are available on the market spice shelf.

The flavors of basil and tomatoes are natural partners. In Italian cookery, basil is one of the important seasonings in a variety of tomato-pasta dishes.

Mushroom Pasta Sauce

 1 cup chopped onion
 1 clove garlic, minced
 2 tablespoons olive or salad oil
 2 8-ounce cans tomato sauce
 1 6-ounce can broiled chopped
   mushrooms, undrained
   (1⅓ cups)
 3 tablespoons snipped parsley
 1 tablespoon sugar
 1 teaspoon dried basil, crushed
 ½ teaspoon salt.

Cook onion and garlic in hot oil till tender but not brown. Add tomato sauce, mushrooms with liquid, parsley, sugar, basil, and salt. Mix together thoroughly.

Simmer uncovered about 45 minutes or till of desired consistency. Serve over hot spaghetti or other pasta. Pass grated Parmesan cheese to sprinkle atop. Makes 4 to 6 servings.

Basil Carrots

 2 tablespoons butter
 6 medium carrots, thinly sliced
   on bias
 ¼ teaspoon salt
 ¼ teaspoon dried basil, crushed

In medium skillet melt butter. Add carrots; sprinkle with salt and crushed basil. Cover and simmer 10 to 12 minutes or till carrots are tender. Makes 6 servings.

Simmered Beef Shanks

 2 tablespoons all-purpose flour
 1 tablespoon salt
 ¼ teaspoon pepper
 3 to 4 pounds crosscut beef
   shanks
 1 tablespoon shortening
 1 cup tomato juice
 2 tablespoons snipped parsley
 ½ teaspoon dried basil, crushed
 4 medium potatoes, peeled and
   quartered
 ½ cup cold water
 2 tablespoons all-purpose flour

Combine 2 tablespoons flour, salt, and pepper in a paper or plastic bag; add beef shanks, one at a time, and shake to coat. Brown meat in hot shortening in Dutch oven. Add tomato juice, parsley, and basil. Cover and simmer 1½ hours. Add potatoes; cover and simmer 30 to 45 minutes more or till potatoes are tender. Remove meat and potatoes; skim off excess fat from pan juices.

Add enough water to juices to make 1 cup liquid; return to pan. In small mixing bowl blend together cold water and 2 tablespoons flour; stir into juices. Cook and stir till thickened and bubbly. Serve hot with beef shanks and potatoes. Makes 4 to 6 servings.

Use basil to lend a pleasant flavor to vegetables such as peas, squash, carrots, eggplant, string beans, potatoes, and spinach. Perk up tossed salads by sprinkling crushed basil over the salad or adding it to French or Russian dressing. Flavor Manhattan clam chowder, minestrone, bean, turtle, and beef soups as well as lamb and veal stews with basil leaves. For a delightful spicy taste in seafood, add a few fresh or dried basil leaves to the liquid used to cook fish or shellfish.

The basil flavor also adds a special touch to scrambled eggs, lamb, venison, beef, liver, and all types of poultry.

Because the pleasant, spicy flavor of basil blends so well with such a variety of dishes, many cooks consider basil an essential herb. If substituting fresh basil for dried, use about 3 times more of the fresh herb. (See also *Herb*.)

BASS—Many-specied, edible fish with spiny fins and rough scales. They vary in size, according to species, from one-half pound to more than 100 pounds.

Bass is a fresh and saltwater fish. A number of varieties inhabit the ocean as well as streams and lakes. Black sea bass come from Atlantic waters; white sea bass are found in the Pacific Ocean. Inland rivers or lakes are sources of varieties like calico, white, channel, striped, and largemouth or smallmouth black bass.

Fresh or frozen bass are marketed or can be cut in a number of forms depending on the size of the fish. The smallest are usually used whole; medium-sized, filleted; and the largest, cut into steaks. The delicate-flavored meat is suitable for a variety of cooking methods—baking, boiling, broiling or frying. (See also *Fish.*)

BASTE—To pour or brush flavorful liquid onto foods during cooking. Baste and brush are similar terms with a minor difference. Brushing may be done before, during, or after the cooking process; basting is done only while the food cooks.

Basting helps to keep food moist, to brown or glaze attractively, and to add flavor. The liquids most commonly used include pan drippings, fruit or vegetable juices, highly seasoned sauces, and fruity or sweet glaze mixtures.

Basting liquids can be applied with a pastry brush or long-handled barbecue brush; poured on with a spoon, ladle, or cup; or squeezed on with a bulb-baster syringe, made for that purpose. (See *Brush, Glaze* for additional information.)

BATTER—A pourable mixture composed of flour and liquid such as milk. The addition of eggs, sugars, shortenings, and leavening agents produces many different mixtures which can be referred to as batters. While each can have its distinctive characteristics, in general they fall into two categories: pour and drop batters.

Pour batters are those prepared for pancakes, popovers, and waffles. For each cup of liquid used, there is usually one cup, more or less, of flour. This type of batter is thin enough in consistency to pour in a steady stream.

Coating batter, a pour batter, is used as a covering for foods to be fried. The pieces of food should be well dried before being dipped so that the batter will cling during frying. Cooked coating batter has delightful crisp texture.

Drop batters, the second type, break into soft clumps when poured or spooned. These batters are used to make drop biscuits and cookies, muffins, fritters, and cakes. For each cup of liquid used, there are about two cups of flour.

In some batters, the liquid is added to sifted dry ingredients all at once. Mixing is quick since over-mixing, particularly in heavier drop batters, tends to toughen the baked product. (See also *Dough.*)

BATTER BREAD—A yeast bread that is vigorously beaten but not kneaded. These are sometimes called no-knead breads.

The baked texture of batter breads is fairly coarse. No kneading and quick rising allow them to be made and baked in a relatively short time. (See also *Bread.*)

Batter Rolls

3¼ cups sifted all-purpose flour
1 package active dry yeast
• • •
1¼ cups milk
½ cup shortening
¼ cup sugar
1 slightly beaten egg

In large mixer bowl combine *2 cups* flour and yeast. Heat milk, shortening, sugar, and 1 teaspoon salt just till warm, stirring occasionally to melt shortening. Add to flour mixture; add egg.

Beat on low speed of electric mixer ½ minute or till gluten strands are practically visible. Beat 3 minutes at high speed of electric mixer. Add remaining flour.

Beat batter at medium speed until smooth, about 2 minutes. Since batter is stiff, you might need to push it away from beaters with a rubber scraper occasionally. Cover dough and let rise till double, about 1 hour. Stir down and beat thoroughly with a wooden spoon. Make batter mixture into Dinner Rolls or Butterscotch Dainties. For Cinnamon Nut Whirls chill dough overnight.

Dinner Rolls

Prepare batter as directed in Batter Rolls. After batter has risen, stir down. Drop batter by tablespoons into 2¾-inch greased muffin pans, filling them half full. Let rise in warm place till double, about 30 minutes. Bake rolls at 400° about 15 minutes.

Butterscotch Dainties

    1 recipe Batter Rolls
  2¼ cups light corn syrup
  1½ cups brown sugar
   ¾ cup butter or margarine
  36 pecan halves

Prepare batter as directed. In skillet combine syrup, sugar, and butter; heat slowly, stirring often. Place 2 teaspoons hot mixture into each 2-inch muffin cup. Place nut half on top.

After batter has risen, stir down; drop into cups, filling half full. Let rise till double. Bake at 375° for 15 to 20 minutes. Cool 2 to 3 minutes. Invert; remove pan. Makes 36.

Cinnamon Nut Whirls

Prepare 1 recipe Batter Rolls. Chill overnight. To shape, combine 1 cup sugar, 1 cup finely chopped nuts, and 2 teaspoons ground cinnamon. Spread mixture on waxed paper.

Grease hands; roll dough into 8-inch strands about ½ inch thick. Coat strands with sugar-nut mixture. Coil on greased baking sheet. Let rise till light, about 30 minutes. Bake at 375° for 15 to 20 minutes. Makes 18.

BAVARIAN CREAM—A delicate molded dessert made from custard, gelatin, and whipped cream. Fruit and fruit juices give Bavarians luscious flavor and color; but crushed candies, ground nuts, sweet wines and liqueurs are also used if a more exotic flavor is desired. Bavarian creams are often served with a sauce.

The origin of Bavarian creams has never been clearly determined, but they were frequently served during the middle and late nineteenth century. (See *Custard, Dessert, Gelatin* for additional information.)

Raspberry Bavarian Mold

A simplified yet elegant version—

  1 6-ounce can (⅔ cup)
    evaporated milk
  1 10-ounce package frozen red
    raspberries, thawed

     · · ·

  2 4-serving envelopes low-calorie
    raspberry-flavored gelatin
  1 cup boiling water
  1 tablespoon lemon juice
    Dash salt

Pour evaporated milk into freezer tray. Freeze till soft ice crystals form around edges. Meanwhile, take out 2 tablespoons of raspberries with syrup; save for garnish. Drain remaining berries, reserving syrup.

Dissolve gelatin in boiling water; add reserved syrup, lemon juice, and salt. Chill till partially set. Add icy cold milk; beat at high speed till soft peaks form, about 4 minutes. Fold in drained raspberries. Pour into 6½-cup mold. Chill till firm.

Unmold onto serving platter; drizzle reserved raspberries over top. Makes 6 servings.

To avoid a last minute rush at bridge club, make Raspberry Bavarian Mold in advance. Then simply unmold, garnish, and serve.

BAVAROISE *(ba va rwäz')*—A French term used to describe a once-popular hot beverage made of eggs and sweet, milky tea flavored with brandy or rum.

BAY LEAF—The leaf of the sweet bay tree used to season food. A member of the laurel family, the trees are evergreens with smooth, shiny, stiff green leaves and are grown in Turkey, Greece, Portugal, and Yugoslavia. It should be noted that the bay leaves used in cooking have nothing to do with the bay leaf of the myrtle family from which bay rum is made. Neither should they be confused with leaves of the mountain laurel or the ornamental American laurel which are not used in food.

Because bay leaf is an herb known in antiquity, legends and myths about its wonderful powers abound. One Greek myth tells that this evergreen tree was once a beautiful nymph. She was turned into a tree to escape the unwelcome advances of the god of the sun, Apollo. Because this tree was beloved by Apollo, no harm could ever come to the tree, or to those who stayed near it. It was thought that mortals seeking shelter under its branches during a storm would be protected from lightning.

Bay leaves have an elusive and delicious aroma. Their uses in cooking throughout the world are many. Meats, especially pot roasts, benefit from the flavor of bay leaf. Stews, many vegetables, soups, and sauces for fish are enhanced by its judicious use. Bay leaves are a basic ingredient in a bouquet garni prized by famous chefs everywhere. This herb is also important in pickle making and the production of vinegar.

Like many other natural products, whole bay leaves will vary in size from one to three inches. The medium-sized leaf, two inches in length, is the guide to use when a recipe specifies "a bay leaf." This amount of the herb is right for flavoring about six servings of food.

Following recipe directions regarding when to add the leaf and how long it is simmered in the mixture is important. Bay leaf is always removed before the cooked food is served, but many recipes specify discarding it at some point earlier in the cooking process. (See also *Herb.*)

Short Rib Stew

Brown slowly 2 to 3 pounds beef short ribs on all sides in Dutch oven; drain off excess fat. Season with salt and pepper; add enough water to almost cover meat. Cover; simmer for 2 to 2½ hours or till meat is tender.

Add 2 medium onions, quartered; 2 medium potatoes, peeled and cubed; 1 medium rutabaga, peeled and cubed; 4 medium carrots, peeled and cut in 1-inch pieces; 2 teaspoons Worcestershire sauce; and 1 bay leaf. Season with salt and pepper. Cover; simmer 20 to 30 minutes or till tender. Discard bay leaf. Remove meat and vegetables from Dutch oven and transfer to serving dish; keep warm while preparing gravy.

Skim excess fat from pan juices. Combine ½ cup cold water with ¼ cup all-purpose flour; stir into pan juices. Cook, stirring till thick and bubbly. Spoon gravy atop stew. Serves 6.

Pork Chop Oven Dinner

       6 pork chops, about ¾ inch
          thick
       3 tablespoons all-purpose flour
     ¾ teaspoon salt
     ¼ teaspoon garlic salt
     ½ cup water
     ¼ cup dry sherry
       1 tablespoon snipped parsley
     ⅛ teaspoon ground cloves
          Dash pepper
       1 bay leaf
       6 small carrots, peeled and
          halved lengthwise
       6 small potatoes, peeled and
          halved
       1 medium onion, thinly sliced

Trim fat from chops. Heat fat in skillet. When 2 tablespoons melted fat accumulate, remove trimmings. Combine flour, salt, dash pepper, and garlic salt; dip chops in mixture. Brown chops in hot fat, about 15 minutes per side.

In 3-quart casserole, combine water and next 5 ingredients. Sprinkle carrots and potatoes generously with salt; *place in the liquid.* Arrange pork chops atop; add onion slices. Cover. Bake at 350° for 1¼ hours or till vegetables and meat are tender, basting once or twice. Skim off excess fat; remove bay leaf. Trim with parsley, if desired. Makes 6 servings.

Tufoli Stuffed with Veal

    1 16-ounce can tomatoes, cut up
    1 cup tomato juice
    1 8-ounce can tomato sauce
    ½ cup chopped onion
    1 teaspoon Worcestershire
        sauce
    1 clove garlic, crushed
    ¼ teaspoon dried thyme leaves,
        crushed
    ¼ teaspoon dried marjoram leaves,
        crushed
    1 bay leaf
    4 ounces tufoli *or* large tubular
        macaroni
    ¼ cup milk
    1 slightly beaten egg
    ¼ cup chopped onion
    ½ teaspoon dried oregano leaves,
        crushed
    1 teaspoon salt
    1 pound ground veal

In saucepan combine first 9 ingredients. Bring to boiling; reduce heat. Simmer mixture, uncovered, 30 minutes. Cook tufoli in boiling, salted water till tender. Drain; cool. Combine dash pepper and remaining ingredients except veal. Add veal, mix well. Stuff into tufoli. Pour *half* the sauce into 12x7½x2-inch baking dish. Arrange stuffed tufoli over sauce; cover with remaining sauce. Cover; bake at 350° for 1 hour. Makes 6 to 8 servings.

Eggs in Spanish Sauce

In saucepan melt 3 tablespoons butter. Add ½ cup chopped onion; cook till tender. Blend in 3 tablespoons all-purpose flour, 2 teaspoons sugar, ¾ teaspoon salt, and dash pepper. Add one 28-ounce can tomatoes, cut up, and 1 small bay leaf. Cook, stirring constantly, till thick and bubbly. Remove bay leaf. Pour into 10x6x 1½-inch baking dish.

Halve 6 hard-cooked eggs lengthwise. Remove yolks; mash with ¼ cup mayonnaise, 1 teaspoon prepared mustard, ⅛ teaspoon salt, and dash pepper. Refill whites and arrange in baking dish. Combine ¾ cup fine dry bread crumbs and 2 tablespoons melted butter; sprinkle atop eggs. Bake at 425° for 10 minutes or till hot. Serve over noodles. Serves 6.

Spicy Whole Tomatoes

    ¼ cup butter or margarine
    ½ cup chopped onion
    2 tablespoons brown sugar
    6 whole cloves
    2 bay leaves, crumbled
    2 inches stick cinnamon,
        broken in pieces
    1½ teaspoons salt
        Dash freshly ground pepper
    6 medium tomatoes, peeled
        and cored

In skillet melt butter. Add chopped onion, brown sugar, cloves, crumbled bay leaves, cinnamon pieces, salt, and pepper. Cook till onion is tender. Place the tomatoes cored side down in the skillet and carefully spoon butter mixture over. Cover; simmer 5 minutes. Carefully turn tomatoes. Simmer, uncovered, 5 to 10 minutes longer or till tomatoes are tender, basting often. Serve in sauce dishes. Serves 6.

BEACH PLUM—Fruit of a shrub growing wild along sandy beaches on the eastern seaboard from Virginia to New England. They are small, round, and purple in color with a range in flavor from faintly bitter to tangy-sweet. Although they may be eaten raw, beach plums are usually made into flavorful jams and jellies to be served either as a spread for bread or as a meat accompaniment. (See also *Plum.*)

BEACH STRAWBERRY—A sweet-tasting wild berry that grows along the Pacific coast from California to Alaska. It is also found along the southern coast of Chile and on a few mountain tops in Hawaii. The first cultivated strawberries were developed by crossing the Chilean beach strawberry with the meadow strawberry from the eastern United States. The freshly picked wild beach strawberries may be enjoyed by the bowlful with sugar and cream or made into a delectable strawberry jam. (See also *Strawberry.*)

BEAD MOLASSES—A type of dark molasses used as the base for the brown gravy coloring important in many forms of Chinese cookery. (See also *Molasses.*)

BEAN

*This influential vegetable performs a dual role
—fresh or dried—in the family menu.*

These edible members of the legume family come in many shapes, sizes, and colors —large and small; flat, round, or oval; pink, speckled, brown, black, red, or light green. Green and yellow wax snap beans are really immature seeds in a tender, fleshy pod, to be eaten pod and all. Shell beans have been shucked from the pod and are used in a mature but unripened state or are allowed to fully ripen then dried before being used.

For thousands of years beans have been an important food throughout the world. In the Orient, for example, varieties like the mung bean have long been made into popular foods. Soybeans were Asians' source of protein before the Christian Era.

Cultivated beans of the kidney bean group (snap beans, pintos, white beans), the type familiar to Americans, were developed in this hemisphere. The Incans of Peru first domesticated these bean plants. Central and North American Indians used many of these varieties years before exploration of the New World began.

These Indians produced beans that would grow in substandard soil, dried them for storage, and ate them as a source of high energy. Their importance and significance still survives in Indian customs celebrated by Hopi Indians in their Bean Festival.

American colonists incorporated many Indian foods into their diets because the foods were tasty and plentiful. Beans soon became a traditional basis for regional dishes throughout the country: succotash (Indians called it misickquatash), Boston baked beans, chili, refried beans. Pioneers rapidly learned that the dried beans' keeping quality was ideal for an adventurous traveler's food supplies.

As early as the 1800s, beans were produced commercially. Variety developments included the introduction of stringless beans in 1894. Fresh string beans, now stringless, became known as snap beans for when bent in half with the fingers, fresh green or yellow beans snap easily.

How beans are produced: Bean plants are grown annually from seeds. Some plants are bushy and low to the ground; others, the "pole" beans, may climb as high as seven feet, entwining themselves around poles or other plants. For the most part, plants grown for their dry seeds develop pods too tough for eating while edible-podded varieties produce mature seeds low in eating quality.

The bean plant structure makes it suitable for mechanical harvesting. The seeds or beans grown in pods are marked lengthwise by seams. Fresh or shell beans are picked before the pods split, while beans for drying are completely mature before they are harvested.

Where beans are produced most numerously depends on the weather and soil conditions necessary for the variety. Many types are frost susceptible and harmed by extremely hot weather. Most beans processed by drying are grown only where commercially profitable. Leading producers include California, Michigan, Idaho, Colorado and Nebraska. Podded beans are widely grown in New York and Oregon; while lima crops appear throughout California, Delaware, and New Jersey.

Beanstalk favorites

← Shapely jars hold shelled dry beans—speckled pintos, white navy beans, red kidney beans, and green limas. In the foreground are favas with green and wax snap beans.

Dry beans

A wide flavor and texture assortment of dry beans is available, plain or processed. Use them in new or traditional bean dishes to transform meal plans into imaginative and delicious as well as budget-wise and nutritious realities.

Nutritional value: The dry beans are substantially higher in protein than fresh beans or other vegetables. Although of good quality, the protein is incomplete nutritionally until combined with protein from an animal source. When some meat, egg, or cheese is added to a recipe or menu, the protein value is excellent.

Dried beans fall into the meat class of food groups. One cup of cooked dried beans provides a good occasional substitute for two to three ounces of lean cooked meat. Furthermore, all dry beans are sources of thiamine, other B vitamins, and iron.

Types of dry beans: Dry bean varieties are used extensively over the globe. Soybeans are the world's most important beans. They are highly nutritious yet an inexpensive food source of protein for underdeveloped countries. Garbanzo beans or chickpeas, a crop of Mediterranean areas and central Asia, are used in soups, stews, and salads. In Swedish settlements, brown beans are in great demand. Black or yellow-eyed peas, really beans, traditionally appear in the southern United States. Light-green limas are a national favorite.

The largest and second most widely cultivated bean group is the kidney bean. All of its species are kidney shaped, but each varies in size and color and is frequently more popular in one region of this country than in another. Black beans, for instance, are grown and eaten mainly in the South; whereas small, round, white pea beans, navy beans, and large white great northern beans are preferred by Northerners. Beige pintos dappled with brown are one of the Southwest's versatile strains.

The dark red kidney beans, however, are both nationally and internationally famous. Identified by their red-purple color and distinctive flavor, they find wide use in salads, soups, and main dishes.

How to select and store: Choose the variety most popular with the family or typical of the dish being prepared. Dried beans are usually prepackaged; but if beans by the pound are available, check cleanliness and even size. Where preparation time is important, purchase processed beans, either canned, frozen, or precooked dried, to achieve faster yet tasty end-products.

Keep opened packages of beans in tightly-covered containers placed in a cool, dry place. If this type of storage is not possible, purchase only in the quantities that are presently needed.

How to prepare: Dry beans require longer cooking time than fresh vegetables due to the water lost in drying and the time needed to soften their structure. For this reason, all dry beans are soaked in water to absorb some liquid before cooking. For 1 cup large white great northern beans use 2½ cups water; for 1 cup pink, brown, red, or pinto beans use 3 cups water.

The preparation method used can markedly improve the quality of cooked beans. First, beans will rehydrate faster in hot water than cold water; but where time is not paramount, either method proves satisfactory. To soak beans quickly, place the rinsed beans in a heavy saucepan or kettle with an amount of water recommended by the recipe or on the package. Bring to boiling. Boil 2 minutes; remove from heat and cover. Soak 1 hour.

To soak beans overnight, pour the measured amount of *cold* water over the rinsed beans. Cover and let stand overnight in a cool place. If this method of rehydration is used during warm weather, the beans should be allowed to stand in the refrigerator to prevent souring.

Minerals which cause hard water can appreciably increase the cooking time needed for dried beans. If excessively hard water, add one-fourth teaspoon baking soda per pound of beans during soaking. Never add soda above this level as the flavor and nutritive value will be adversely affected.

Highly acid foods such as tomatoes, lemon juice, vinegar, and wine also can delay the development of tender bean texture. Wait until the beans are fairly tender before adding these kinds of foods.

Soaked beans are covered tightly and simmered until tender in the kettle (using the soaking liquid, of course, to retain vitamins and minerals). Simmer gently rather than boil the beans to help them retain their shape. The use of about one teaspoon salt per cup of dry beans in the cooking liquid is usually an adequate seasoning level. If salty foods like ham or salt pork are cooked with the beans, wait to add the salt for seasoning until the cooking is almost completed. Also, adding one tablespoon butter or salad oil per cup of beans to the water prevents excessive foaming.

Beans for baked dishes should be cooked only until *almost* tender. For other bean dishes, except where mashed or puréed, cook till the beans are tender but still retain their shape. Avoid overstirring during cooking to keep them whole.

Since beans pick up water in cooking, they puff up greatly. In general, one cup of dried beans (one-half pound) makes 2¼ to 2½ cups cooked beans depending on the variety. The number of servings each cup of cooked beans will yield depends on how the beans are to be used—entrée, appetizer, side dish—and the additional ingredients used in the recipe.

How to use: Widespread popularity of baked beans overshadows the many ways dried beans can be prepared and served. In certain nationalities, for example Mexican, beans are a staple ingredient for vegetable side dishes and main dishes. In this country, beans make appetizing dips and salads or steaming soups and casseroles.

There have been endless discussions about baked beans. Which beans are preferred for baking and how they are seasoned and baked varies from one region of the United States to another. Bostonians most often bake pea beans; though yellow-eyed beans are preferred in Rhode Island and navy beans, in most other parts of New England. In Michigan, white or kidney beans are used; in the South, red beans; and in the Southwest, pintos. Pennsylvanians bake white marrows and also navy beans, kidney beans, and dried limas.

Regional seasonings differ, too. The traditional Boston baked beans are flavored with both brown sugar and molasses, a touch of dry mustard, and a chunk of salt pork—but never with tomato. In Pennsylvania and some other areas, people like their beans baked with tomato juice or tomato catsup. Some cooks prefer the flavor of bacon rather than salt pork, especially when dry limas are baked.

Vermont and New Hampshire baked beans must be flavored with these states' famous maple syrup or sugar. Onion, whole or chopped, is often plunged into the beans to add its flavor.

Traditional baked beans began as an example of Yankee thrift. Dry beans, salt pork, and molasses were all good keepers, always at hand to use for hot and hearty dishes. Beans tasted best when baked slowly for a long time; so after the bread was baked in the morning, the beans were set on the fire—no sense wasting the gradually lessening heat in the fireplace oven.

Homemakers who couldn't take time away from other jobs gave their bean pots to the local baker on Saturday morning. In the evening, the baked beans were returned with some traditional brown bread.

Saturday night supper was ready in either case when mealtime came around, and the reheated leftover beans were fine breakfast fare for Sunday morning. The custom of baked beans for Saturday night and Sunday morning is still observed in many homes, especially in New England.

New England Baked Beans

Rinse 1 pound (2 cups) dried navy beans. Combine beans and 8 cups cold water in kettle. Bring to boiling. Simmer 2 minutes; remove from heat. Cover; let stand 1 hour. (Or, add beans to cold water; soak overnight.)

Add ½ teaspoon salt to beans and water. Cover; simmer till tender, about 1 hour. Drain, reserving liquid. Measure 2 cups liquid adding water if needed; mix with ½ cup molasses, ⅓ cup brown sugar, and 1 teaspoon dry mustard.

Cut ¼ pound salt pork in half. Score one half; set aside. Grind or thinly slice remainder. In 2-quart bean pot or casserole combine beans; 1 medium onion, sliced; and ground salt pork. Pour sugar-bean liquid over. Top with scored pork. Cover; bake at 300° for 5 to 7 hours. Add more liquid, if needed. Serves 8.

For home-baked beans the traditional way, take time to simmer the beans until tender. Don't hurry them up by boiling. This tends to toughen the beans and to induce bursting—then they become mushy.

Hearty Baked Beans

1½ cups dry navy beans
1½ cups dry baby limas
1 large onion, chopped (1 cup)
1 teaspoon salt
2 whole bay leaves
½ teaspoon dried thyme leaves, crushed
¼ teaspoon pepper
1 1½- to 2-pound boneless smoked pork shoulder (picnic)
1 19-ounce can tomatoes
2 cups sliced celery
⅓ cup dark corn syrup

Rinse beans; cover with 6 cups cold water in large kettle. Bring to boiling; simmer 2 minutes. Remove from heat. Cover; let stand 1 hour. Stir in chopped onion, salt, bay leaves, thyme, and pepper. Add meat; cover and simmer for about 1 hour.

Remove meat; let stand till cool enough to cut. Dice, discarding fat. Combine beans, meat, tomatoes, sliced celery, and dark corn syrup; turn into 2½-quart bean pot or casserole. Bake covered at 350° for 2 hours. Uncover; bake 2 hours more, stirring several times. Remove bay leaves. Makes 8 to 10 servings.

Many beans served nowadays are slow-baked commercially and canned in varieties to suit every taste. For quick baked beans, use canned beans of the kind and flavor desired, then add seasoning touches.

Easy Baked Beans

4 slices bacon
½ cup chopped onion
2 tablespoons brown sugar
1 tablespoon Worcestershire sauce
1 teaspoon prepared mustard
2 16-ounce cans (4 cups) pork and beans in tomato sauce

In skillet cook bacon till crisp; drain, reserving 2 tablespoons drippings. Crumble bacon and set aside. Cook onion in reserved drippings till tender but not brown; add onions, crumbled bacon, sugar, Worcestershire sauce, and mustard to pork and beans. Mix well. Turn into 1½-quart bean pot or casserole. Bake uncovered at 325° for 1½ to 1¾ hours. Serves 6.

Rancho Bean Casserole

½ pound ground beef
• • •
1 16-ounce can (2 cups) pork and beans in tomato sauce
1 16-ounce can dark red kidney beans, drained
½ cup water
⅓ cup catsup
½ envelope dry onion soup mix
1 tablespoon prepared mustard

Brown ground beef; drain. Stir in remaining ingredients. Turn into 1½-quart casserole. Bake covered at 350° for 1 hour. Serves 6 to 8.

Potluck Bean Bake

1 16-ounce can (2 cups) beans in barbecue sauce
1 16-ounce can cut green beans, drained
1 8-ounce can (1 cup) limas with ham
1 teaspoon instant minced onion

Combine all ingredients in 1½ quart casserole. Bake at 350° for about 1½ hours. Let stand 10 minutes before serving. Makes 8 servings.

Apple-Bean Bake

Turn two 16-ounce cans (4 cups) pork and beans in tomato sauce into 1½-quart casserole. Combine ¼ cup light molasses, 2 tablespoons vinegar, and 2 tablespoons prepared mustard; blend into beans. Gently stir *half* of a 20-ounce can pie-sliced apples, drained, into bean mixture.

Arrange remaining apple slices on top. Cover and bake at 350° for 1½ hours. Uncover and bake 30 minutes longer. Makes 6 to 8 servings.

Orange Baked Beans

  2 16-ounce cans (4 cups) pork and
      beans in tomato sauce
  ½ cup brown sugar
  ¼ cup catsup
  3 tablespoons frozen orange juice
      concentrate, thawed
  1 tablespoon instant minced onion
  ½ teaspoon Worcestershire sauce

Stir together beans, brown sugar, catsup, orange juice concentrate, onion, and Worcestershire sauce in saucepan. Bring to boiling; reduce heat and simmer uncovered for 10 minutes, stirring occasionally. Makes 6 to 8 servings.

Maple Baked Beans

  6 slices bacon
  2 16-ounce cans (4 cups) pork and
      beans in tomato sauce
  ½ cup chopped celery
  ½ cup catsup
  ½ cup maple-flavored syrup
  1 tablespoon instant minced onion
  1 tablespoon prepared mustard

Cook bacon till crisp; drain, reserving 2 tablespoons drippings. Crumble bacon. Combine bacon and reserved drippings with remaining ingredients. Turn into 10x6x1½-inch baking dish. Bake at 350° for 1¼ hours. Serves 4 to 6.

This country's forefathers are to be thanked for developing all-time favorites like New England Baked Beans. To follow the local custom, serve this dish with Boston brown bread.

Build a storehouse of bean recipes and ideas using dried beans in their natural or processed form. For a hearty meal-in-a-dish, combine canned baked beans with sliced frankfurters or smoked pork chops in a casserole. Use leftover baked beans for satisfying sandwiches, or just make bean sandwiches because they're so good. A soup or stew starts out right when beans are included. (See also *Vegetable*.)

Calico Bean Bake

    1 cup chopped onion
    1 clove garlic, minced
    1 tablespoon shortening
        •   •   •
    1 16-ounce can (2 cups) pork
        and beans in tomato sauce
    1 16-ounce can kidney beans,
        drained
    1 16-ounce can baby limas,
        drained
    ½ cup catsup
    2 tablespoons brown sugar
    1 to 2 tablespoons vinegar
    1 teaspoon salt
    1 teaspoon dry mustard

In skillet cook onion and garlic in shortening till tender. Add beans, catsup, brown sugar, vinegar, salt, and mustard. Turn into 1½-quart casserole. Bake at 350° for 1½ hours. Serves 6.

Kettle-of-Bean Stew

Makes good use of a leftover ham bone—

In Dutch oven bring 1½ cups dry navy beans and 4½ cups water to boil; reduce heat. Simmer 2 minutes. Remove from heat; let stand 1 hour. Drain beans, reserving liquid. Add enough water to liquid to make 3½ cups.

In Dutch oven, combine reserved liquid; beans; 1 meaty ham bone *or* 2 cups small pieces cooked ham; 1 medium onion, sliced; ½ teaspoon salt; 1 whole bay leaf (optional); and dash pepper. Heat to boiling; reduce heat. Cover and simmer 2¼ hours. (If using ham bone, remove; cut off any meat then return meat to stew.) Uncover; continue cooking 15 minutes more. Makes 4 servings.

Chicken-Vegetable Chowder

    4 cups water
    1 16-ounce can kidney beans,
        drained
    1 16-ounce can mixed vegetables,
        drained
    1 8-ounce can tomatoes, cut up
    1 envelope dry tomato-vegetable
        soup mix
    2 5-ounce cans boned chicken

In large saucepan combine water, beans, mixed vegetables, tomatoes, and dry soup mix. Add chicken. Heat to boiling; reduce heat and simmer uncovered for 10 minutes. Serves 8.

Egg and Bean Salad

    1 16-ounce can barbecue beans,
        drained
    6 hard-cooked eggs, coarsely
        chopped
    ¼ cup chopped onion
        •   •   •
    1 tablespoon mayonnaise or salad
        dressing
    1 teaspoon prepared mustard
    ¼ teaspoon salt
    3 slices bacon, crisp-cooked and
        crumbled

Combine beans, eggs, and onion. Chill. Blend together mayonnaise, mustard, salt, and dash pepper. Add to egg mixture and toss. Spoon into lettuce-lined salad bowl. Sprinkle crumbled bacon over top. Makes 6 to 8 servings.

Barbecued Bean Bake

Cut one 7-ounce can luncheon meat into 2 or 3 slices. Pour one 16-ounce can baked beans and pork in molasses sauce into small baking dish. Mix 2 tablespoons brown sugar, 2 tablespoons catsup, and 1 tablespoon prepared mustard. Spread some of mixture on meat and mix remaining into beans. Arrange meat atop beans in baking dish.

With wooden pick, attach 1 thin slice onion and ½ slice lemon to each luncheon meat slice. Bake at 375° for 35 to 40 minutes or till mixture is hot. Makes 2 servings.

Three-Bean Frank Bake

    1 pound frankfurters, sliced
    1 16-ounce can pork and beans in
        tomato sauce
    1 16-ounce can butter beans,
        drained
    1 16-ounce can red beans
    ½ cup brown sugar
    ½ cup chopped onion
    2 tablespoons wine vinegar
    ¼ teaspoon dried oregano leaves,
        crushed.

Combine all ingredients. Turn into 2½-quart casserole. Bake uncovered at 350° for 2 hours, stirring occasionally. Makes 8 to 10 servings.

Wiener-Bean Bake

    1 10-ounce package frozen limas
    1 16-ounce can (2 cups) pork and
        beans in tomato sauce
    1 16-ounce can kidney beans,
        drained
    1 pound (8 to 10) frankfurters,
        cut in 1-inch pieces
    ½ cup chili sauce
    ¼ cup molasses
    ½ envelope dry onion soup mix
    ½ to 1 teaspoon dry mustard
    ½ teaspoon Worcestershire sauce

Cook limas according to package directions; drain. Mix with remaining ingredients. Turn into 2-quart casserole or bean pot. Bake covered at 350° for 1 hour. Uncover; stir and continue baking 30 minutes. Makes 6 servings.

Boston Beanwich

Butter one side of a whole wheat bread slice. Turn over and spread with ¼ cup drained, canned baked beans in molasses sauce. Crumble 2 slices crisp-cooked bacon over beans. Top with slice of sharp process American cheese.

    Spread second slice of bread with prepared mustard and place atop cheese, mustard side down. Butter the top of sandwich.

    Grill both sides till baked beans are heated through and cheese melts slightly. Serve with sweet pickles. Makes 1 serving.

Bayou Bean-Burgers

    1 16-ounce can kidney beans,
        drained
    ¼ cup finely chopped onion
    ¼ cup sweet pickle relish
    ¾ cup shredded sharp process
        American cheese
    1 tablespoon prepared mustard
       • • •
    4 hamburger buns
    ¼ cup mayonnaise or salad
        dressing

Combine beans, onion, pickle relish, ¼ *cup* shredded cheese, and mustard. Split buns and toast in broiler. Spread each toasted half with mayonnaise. Cover bottom half of each bun with bean mixture. Top with remaining cheese. Return halves with bean mixture to broiler. Heat till cheese melts. Makes 4 servings.

Hot Mexican Bean Dip

Perfect appetizer for a "taco" party—

    1 28-ounce can (3¼ cups) pork and
        beans in tomato sauce, sieved
    ½ cup shredded sharp process
        American cheese
    2 teaspoons vinegar
    2 teaspoons Worcestershire sauce
    1 teaspoon garlic salt
    1 teaspoon chili powder
    ½ teaspoon salt
    ½ teaspoon liquid smoke
       Dash cayenne pepper
       • • •
    4 slices bacon, crisp-cooked
        and crumbled

Combine all ingredients *except* bacon; heat through. Top with bacon. Serve with corn chips or potato chips. Makes 3 cups.

Fresh beans

Except for shelled limas, fresh beans have different appearance and nutrition characteristics from dried beans. For this reason, they are purchased and prepared in a definitive manner, one that is best suited for fresh beans, shelled or in pods.

Nutritional Value: The food value in snap beans and shell beans differs considerably. Fresh limas contain some protein, about six to eight percent; while snap beans, both green and yellow, have practically none. Limas are also three times higher in carbohydrate than snap beans. The fat of both types, however, is negligible.

Even though they are not major contributors of a particular vitamin or mineral, both snap and lima beans add a good assortment of important nutrients, particularly in the vitamin A and B area, that help maintain a balanced daily diet. Yellow wax beans, because of their lighter color lag behind the green varieties in the amount of vitamin A present.

Types of fresh beans: The fresh bean category subdivides into two groups: beans picked, cooked, and eaten in immature pods (green or yellow wax snap beans), and beans picked in pods but shelled for cooking and eating (fresh limas and favas).

Green and yellow wax snap beans are harvested primarily from varieties that grow in "bush" fashion. Some, like the Kentucky Wonder, are vine or pole beans. Despite these differences, all snap beans can be used interchangeably.

Lima and fava beans have certain appearance similarities; but shelled favas, also called broad beans, are probably least familiar to Americans. Europeans, on the other hand, use them more frequently than any other variety. Fava beans grow in long, round velvety pods that are lima-like in shape but thicker and slightly larger.

How to select: Buying fresh beans needn't be a matter of vegetable likes or dislikes. For tasty changes, make all fresh beans at least occasional menu visitors.

Identify good-quality snap beans by their long, straight pods that are free from blemishes and that snap crisply when bent.

Which salad tastes the best?

← All three win a prize when judged by bean lovers—One Bean Toss with Herbed Carrots, Hot Five Bean Salad, and Four Bean Salad.

Ridges or bulges appearing on the pods mark the more mature beans—too tough and leathery in texture for eating.

The limas and favas selected should be clean, dark green, full-podded, and crisp. The seeds themselves are best when plump, tender-skinned, and green or greenish-white in color. Large limas are often called potato beans; smaller-sized limas may be called butter beans or baby limas.

Most fresh beans are available the entire year, but the peak crops come between spring and fall. If the fresh products cannot be purchased, equally good choices are the frozen and canned beans cut in assorted styles and processed plain or in specialty sauces. These beans save the homemaker's time and taste good, too.

How to store: Like any fresh vegetable, use beans soon after purchase for peak flavor and texture. Fresh beans should be stored whole in plastic bags or containers in the refrigerator until ready for use. Limas and favas should not be shelled until prepared for cooking. The beans will then retain a plumpness and sweet flavor.

How to prepare: Shell limas or cut snap beans taste best when prepared for cooking as near to mealtime as possible. Initial preparation of fresh beans requires that the pods be washed thoroughly in cold water. Ends and strings, if any, are removed from snap bean varieties.

Limas or favas are prepared in exactly the same way—just shell and cook. Snap beans, however, can be prepared whole or cut in one-inch pieces, diagonal slices, or French-style lengthwise slivers.

Fresh beans are then cooked in a small amount of boiling salted water. After adding the beans to the boiling water, leave the saucepan cover off till the water returns to a boil; cover for the remaining cooking time. This lets out a substance found in beans that can change their bright green color to a dull, unappetizing olive if not allowed to escape.

Cooking time will vary with how the snap beans are cut and how large the limas or favas are. In general, whole, one-inch cut pieces, and medium-sized limas require 20 to 30 minutes cooking. French-style beans usually need only 10 to 12 minutes. The most important factor for best cooking results, however, is that the beans be cooked till crisp-tender.

How to use: Whether serving properly cooked beans in their own juice, with flavor additions such as butter, seasonings, and sauces, or in assorted food combinations, fresh or processed beans have tremendous appeal. Savory, an herb known as bean weed in Germany, basil, dill, marjoram, oregano, and tarragon are but a few of the herbaceous flavor touches for snap beans. Bits of ham or bacon cooked with beans lend Southern style to a bean dish. A little sautéed chopped onion or slivers of canned pimiento added to green limas tastefully satisfies the urge to be different.

Hot Five Bean Salad

In large skillet cook 8 slices bacon till crisp; drain, reserving ¼ cup drippings. Crumble bacon; set aside. In skillet combine ⅔ cup sugar, 2 tablespoons cornstarch, 1½ teaspoons salt, and dash pepper with reserved drippings. Stir in ¾ cup vinegar and ½ cup water; heat to boiling, stirring constantly.

Add one 16-ounce can *each* kidney beans, cut green beans, limas, cut wax beans, and garbanzo beans, *all drained.* Reduce heat. Cover; simmer 15 to 20 minutes. Turn into dish. Top with bacon. Makes 10 to 12 servings.

One Bean Toss

Olives are the colorful garnish—

    ½ cup sliced pitted ripe olives
    ¼ cup sliced pimiento-stuffed
        green olives
    1 16-ounce can peas, drained
    1 16-ounce can limas, drained
    ½ cup mayonnaise or salad
        dressing
    2 tablespoons grated onion
    1 tablespoon lemon juice
    1 tablespoon drained capers
    2 teaspoons liquid from capers
        Herbed Carrots
        Parsley

Set aside a few olive slices for garnish; combine remaining olive slices, peas, and limas in bowl. Combine next 5 ingredients, ½ teaspoon salt, and dash pepper; pour over bean mixture and toss lightly. Cover; chill several hours, stirring occasionally.

To serve mound bean salad mixture in center of lettuce-lined platter. Top with reserved olives and additional mayonnaise, if desired. Arrange Herbed Carrots and parsley around. Makes 8 servings.

Herbed Carrots: Place one 16-ounce can whole small carrots, drained, in a deep bowl. Combine ⅓ cup salad oil; 2 tablespoons tarragon vinegar; 2 tablespoons finely snipped parsley; ¼ teaspoon salt; ¼ teaspoon dried thyme leaves, crushed, *or* dried marjoram leaves, crushed; and dash pepper. Pour over carrots. Cover; chill 3 hours, spooning dressing over occasionally. Drain thoroughly.

Four Bean Salad

        Romaine leaves
    1 16-ounce can *each* red kidney
        beans, cut wax beans, black-
        eyed peas *or* limas, cut green
        beans, *all* drained
    1 medium green pepper, thinly
        sliced into rings
    1 medium onion, thinly sliced
        and separated into rings
    ½ cup sugar
    ½ cup wine vinegar
    ½ cup salad oil
    2 tablespoons snipped parsley
    1 teaspoon salt
    ½ teaspoon dry mustard
    ½ teaspoon dried tarragon leaves,
        crushed, *or* 2 teaspoons finely
        snipped fresh tarragon
    ½ teaspoon dried basil leaves,
        crushed, *or* 2 teaspoons
        finely snipped fresh basil

Line large salad bowl with romaine. Layer drained red kidney beans, wax beans, black-eyed peas, green beans, and pepper rings in order given. Top with onion rings. Thoroughly combine sugar, vinegar, oil, parsley, salt, dry mustard, tarragon, and basil. Drizzle over vegetables. Cover; chill, stirring occasionally. Before serving stir, then drain. Serves 12.

Green Beans With Dill Sauce

    1 4-ounce container *whipped*
       cream cheese with pimiento
    1 tablespoon light cream
    ½ teaspoon dillweed
    ¼ teaspoon salt
    1 9-ounce package frozen
       French-style green beans

Blend together cream cheese, cream, dillweed, and salt. Cook beans according to package directions; drain. Pour sauce over; toss lightly to melt cheese. Makes 4 servings.

Caraway Green Beans

    ½ cup dairy sour cream
    2 tablespoons all-purpose flour
    2 tablespoons finely chopped onion
    1 tablespoon sugar
    ½ teaspoon salt
    Dash pepper
    Dash ground nutmeg
    ½ cup milk
    ¼ pound caraway Cheddar cheese,
       crumbled (1 cup)

       • • •

    2 9-ounce packages frozen *or* 2
       16-ounce cans French-style
       green beans, cooked and
       drained

Blend sour cream and flour. Stir in remaining ingredients *except* green beans. Heat and stir just until cheese melts. Stir in hot drained beans. Heat through. Sprinkle with ground nutmeg. Makes 6 to 8 servings.

Fiesta Wax Beans

    1 16-ounce can cut wax beans
    ⅔ cup diced celery
    2 tablespoons butter or margarine
    1 chicken bouillon cube
    ¼ cup chili sauce

Drain beans, reserving ¼ cup liquid. In saucepan cook celery in butter until tender. Add reserved liquid and bouillon cube. Simmer till bouillon cube is dissolved. Stir in chili sauce and beans. Heat through. Makes 4 servings.

Saucy Vegetable Trio

For sauce combine 1 cup mayonnaise and 2 hard-cooked eggs, chopped. Blend in 3 tablespoons lemon juice, 2 tablespoons minced onion, 1 teaspoon Worcestershire sauce, 1 teaspoon prepared mustard, ¼ teaspoon garlic salt, and dash bottled hot pepper sauce. Heat and stir over *low heat* till heated through.

    Cook according to package directions: one 10-ounce package frozen French-style green beans, one 10-ounce package frozen peas, and one 10-ounce package frozen baby limas. Drain vegetables and mix. Pour hot sauce mixture over. Makes 8 to 10 servings.

Hamburger-Bean Skillet

    1 pound ground beef
    1 16-ounce can cut green beans,
       undrained
    1 10½-ounce can pizza sauce
    2 teaspoons instant minced onion
    1 cup packaged biscuit mix
    ⅓ cup milk

In skillet brown beef; spoon off excess fat. Season with pepper. Stir in beans, pizza sauce, and onion; heat to boiling. Combine biscuit mix and milk; beat vigorously till stiff but sticky, about 20 strokes. Drop by rounded tablespoon atop boiling meat mixture. Cover and simmer about 12 minutes (do not lift cover during cooking). Makes 4 or 5 servings.

Lima-Burger Soup

    1 pound ground beef
    1 16-ounce can lima beans,
       undrained
    1 16-ounce can tomatoes, cut up
    2 cups chopped celery
    ¼ cup snipped parsley
    3 beef bouillon cubes
    ½ teaspoon dried thyme leaves,
       crushed

In saucepan brown meat; drain off fat. Add remaining ingredients, 4 cups water, 1 teaspoon salt, and ⅛ teaspoon pepper. Simmer covered 30 minutes. Remove cover; simmer 15 minutes. Season to taste. Makes 8 servings.

BEAN CURD—Cooked and puréed soybeans formed into a creamy white, bland, custard like cake. Beans curds have been used frequently in oriental cooking because they are an inexpensive source of vegetable protein. The subtle taste, also, can effectively complement stronger-flavored foods.

Bean curds are delicate, perishable, and fragile. Although usually cooked and served as a vegetable, bean curds may be served uncooked as an accompaniment, seasoned with soy sauce. (See *Oriental Cookery, Soybean* for additional information.)

BEAN SPROUT—Tender bleached sprout of a newly germinated mung bean, and occasionally, of a soybean. They lend delicate crispness to oriental dishes.

In certain areas of the United States, fresh bean sprouts can be purchased in an oriental grocery store. Canned ones are available in many supermarkets. (See *Mung Bean, Oriental Cookery, Soybean* for additional information.)

Bacon Oriental

   1 **pound sliced bacon**
   1 **medium onion, sliced**
   1 **cup chopped celery**
   1 **6-ounce can (1⅓ cups) broiled sliced mushrooms**
   2 **tablespoons cornstarch**
   1 **tablespoon soy sauce**
   ½ **teaspoon salt**
     Dash pepper
   1 **16-ounce can bean sprouts, drained (1 cup)**
   1 **cup chopped green pepper**
     Hot cooked rice

Cook bacon till crisp; remove from pan. Drain all *but* 1 tablespoon drippings. Cook onion and celery in drippings till tender but not brown. Drain mushrooms, reserving liquid; add water to liquid to make 1½ cups.

Dissolve cornstarch in ¼ cup cold water; combine with mushroom liquid, soy sauce, salt, and pepper. Add to onion and celery. Cook and stir till mixture is thickened and bubbly. Stir in mushrooms, bean sprouts, and green pepper; heat through. Crumble bacon over top. Serve with hot rice. Makes 6 to 8 servings.

Beef and Egg Foo Yong

   1 **tablespoon cornstarch**
   2 **teaspoons sugar**
   2 **tablespoons soy sauce**
   1 **teaspoon vinegar**
   ½ **pound ground beef**
   6 **well-beaten eggs**
   ½ **16-ounce can bean sprouts, drained (1 cup)**
   ¼ **cup finely chopped onion**
   ¼ **cup finely chopped celery**
   ½ **teaspoon salt**
   1 **tablespoon shortening**
     Hot cooked rice

In small saucepan combine cornstarch and sugar. Gradually blend in 1 cup water, soy sauce, and vinegar. Cook and stir till thickened and bubbly. Cook 1 minute more. Keep warm.

Cook beef in skillet until lightly browned. Drain off fat. Add meat to beaten eggs with bean sprouts, onion, celery, and salt.

Heat shortening on griddle. Using ¼ cup meat-egg mixture for each patty, pour on griddle. Shape patties with a pancake turner by pushing egg back into the patties. When set and brown on one side, turn to brown other side. Serve with hot cooked rice. Pour sauce over patties and rice. Makes 4 or 5 servings.

Oriental Crunch Burgers

   2 **pounds ground beef**
   1½ **teaspoons salt**
   1 **5-ounce can bean sprouts, drained**
   1 **5-ounce can water chestnuts, drained and chopped**
   ¼ **cup chopped green onion**
   2 **tablespoons soy sauce**
   8 **hamburger buns, split and toasted**

Mix meat with salt; shape into 16 thin patties, 4 inches in diameter. Combine bean sprouts, water chestnuts, onion, and soy sauce. Toss together lightly. Place about 2 tablespoons mixture on *eight* of the patties. Cover with remaining patties; seal edges. Broil 3 inches from heat for 6 minutes; turn and broil 6 minutes longer or till done. Serve in toasted hamburger buns. Makes 8 servings.

American Chop Suey

    1 pound ground pork
    1 16-ounce can bean sprouts,
        drained (1 cup)
    1 cup bias-cut celery
    ½ cup coarsely chopped onion
    1 5-ounce can water chestnuts,
        drained and sliced
    1 3-ounce can sliced mushrooms,
        drained (½ cup)
    1 10½-ounce can condensed beef
        broth
    2 tablespoons cornstarch
    2 tablespoons soy sauce
        Hot cooked rice
    ¼ cup toasted slivered almonds

In skillet cook pork till lightly browned. Drain off excess fat. Add bean sprouts, celery, onion, water chestnuts, and mushrooms. Stir in all but ¼ *cup* of the broth. Bring to boiling; reduce heat. Simmer covered for 15 minutes.

Blend cornstarch, soy sauce, and reserved beef broth. Stir into meat-vegetable mixture. Cook and stir till thickened and bubbly. Serve over rice. Sprinkle almonds over. Pass additional soy sauce, if desired. Makes 6 servings.

Tokyo Turkey Toss

    2 cups diced cooked turkey
    1 16-ounce can bean sprouts,
        drained (1 cup)
    1 cup cooked rice
    1 cup chopped celery
    1 cup coarsely shredded carrot
    2 tablespoons chopped green pepper
    ¼ cup French salad dressing
    2 tablespoons soy sauce
    ½ cup mayonnaise or salad
        dressing
    ½ cup toasted slivered almonds
        Lettuce cups

In large bowl combine turkey, bean sprouts, cooked rice, celery, carrot, green pepper, French dressing, soy sauce, ¼ teaspoon salt, and dash pepper; mix well and chill. Just before serving add mayonnaise and almonds; toss together lightly. Serve in lettuce cups; sprinkle each serving with additional toasted almonds, if desired. Makes 6 servings.

Beans Oriental

Combine 2 tablespoons white wine vinegar and 2 teaspoons instant minced onion; let stand 5 minutes. In skillet cook 3 slices bacon till crisp; remove bacon and crumble. To bacon drippings in skillet add vinegar mixture, 1 tablespoon sugar, and ½ teaspoon salt.

Stir in one 16-ounce can cut green beans, drained, and one 16-ounce can bean sprouts, drained. Heat through. Serve topped with crumbled bacon. Makes 6 to 8 servings.

BEAN THREAD—A ground mung bean product, also called cellophane noodle, that is very thin, hard, and opaque. The bean threads, soaked for a few minutes in warm water, are cooked briefly in boiling liquid or combined with a hot food. In cooking, the noodles become translucent, gelatin-like, and slippery.

Bean threads have more texture than flavor but readily absorb the flavor of the ingredients with which they are cooked. Serve them immediately to retain shape and texture. (See *Mung Bean, Oriental Cookery* for additional information.)

BEAR—A massive, edible mammal with coarse heavy fur, somewhat short limbs, and stubby tail. Indians and the early Americans hunted bear as a source of food.

Bear meat can make enjoyable eating when properly prepared. The older animals require marinating for one day in a mixture of vinegar, wine, and seasonings. All fat and tendons should be removed before cooking to avoid any "wild" taste. The cooking method used, like all meats, depends on the cut of meat—roasting or boiling for less tender pieces, broiling and frying for steaks. Use beef cooking charts as a guide. (See *Beef, Marinade, Wild Game,* for additional information.)

BÉARNAISE SAUCE *(ber nāz')*—A classic sauce in French cooking often served with meat, poultry, or fish. The sauce was created in 1835 at a Paris restaurant and was named after Béarn, a French province.

Béarnaise is made with butter and egg yolks like hollandaise sauce but uses vinegar instead of lemon juice in combi-

Béarnaise Sauce may be prepared by the original method. A quicker way is by Blender Béarnaise. For a delicious entrée, use it to sauce grilled or fried meats, poultry, and fish.

nation with wine, shallots, and herbs, particularly tarragon. (See *French Cookery, Sauce* for additional information.)

Béarnaise Sauce

- 3 tablespoons tarragon vinegar
- 1 teaspoon finely chopped shallot *or* green onion
- 4 whole peppercorns, crushed Bouquet Garni*
- 1 tablespoon cold water
- 4 egg yolks
- ½ cup butter or margarine, softened Salt
- 1 teaspoon minced fresh tarragon leaves *or* ¼ teaspoon dried tarragon leaves, crushed

In small saucepan combine tarragon vinegar, finely chopped shallot or green onion, crushed peppercorns, and Bouquet Garni*. Simmer till liquid is reduced to half. Strain through cheesecloth; add cold water to herb liquid.

Beat egg yolks in top of double boiler. (Top of double boiler should *not* be over the water.) Slowly add strained herb liquid. Add a few tablespoons of the butter or margarine to egg yolks; then place over *hot, not boiling*, water. Cook and stir mixture till butter melts and the sauce starts to thicken.

Continue adding butter, a tablespoon at a time, stirring till all the butter has been used and the sauce is smooth and the consistency of thick cream. Remove from heat. Salt to taste then add tarragon. Makes 1 cup sauce.

*To prepare *Bouquet Garni:* Tightly tie a few fresh or dried whole tarragon leaves and chervil leaves in cheesecloth.

Blender Béarnaise

Place 2 egg yolks, 1 tablespoon lemon juice, 1 teaspoon fresh tarragon leaves *or* ¼ teaspoon dried tarragon leaves, and 1 teaspoon tarragon vinegar in blender container. Turn on and off to combine. With blender at highest speed, *very gradually* add ¾ cup hot melted butter in slow, steady stream. Fold in 2 tablespoons snipped parsley and 1 tablespoon capers, drained and mashed. Garnish with parsley. Makes ¾ cup.

BEAT—To combine briskly with a spoon, whisk, rotary beater, or electric mixer. Beating, like whipping, lightens and smooths, as well as mixes.

The extent to which a food is beaten depends on the recipe itself. This motion can aerate egg white, develop gluten in bread dough, or break up lumps to smooth a batter. (See also *Whip.*)

BEATEN BISCUIT—A brittle, crackerlike biscuit popular in the South prior to the Civil War. Its distinctive hard and crumbly structure is produced by beating the dough before cutting and baking.

The original beaten biscuit recipes contained flour, shortening, and water but no leavening agent. The leavening was achieved by extensive beating. Today, self-rising flour is often used to replace the laborious beating. (See also *Biscuit.*)

Decorate Beaten Biscuits in the traditional manner by pricking the biscuit tops several times with a fork.

Beaten Biscuits

Distinctive texture all their own—

> 2 cups stirred self-rising all-
>   purpose flour
> 1 tablespoon sugar
> ¼ cup shortening
> ⅔ cup water

Blend flour and sugar in mixing bowl. Cut in shortening till mixture appears mealy. Add water, a little at a time; stir to make a stiff dough. Turn out on lightly-floured surface; knead 15 to 20 times, then pound with flat side of mallet 2 to 3 minutes.

Roll dough ½ inch thick; cut in 2-inch rounds. Place biscuits on ungreased baking sheet. Prick tops with fork. Bake at 400° for 20 minutes or till lightly browned. Makes about 1 dozen biscuits.

BÉCHAMEL SAUCE (*ba' she mel'*) — The French name for a basic white sauce that uses milk as the liquid and is closely related to the Velouté Sauce. Béchamel was given its name during the reign of Louis XIV to honor Louis de Béchamel, the head steward for the royal family.

Béchamel is often enriched by the addition of other ingredients, such as butter and cream. Each variation has a definite name. For example, when eggs and cream are added, it is called Parisienne Sauce; a cheese addition is a Mornay Sauce; and when tomato puree is used, it's Aurore Sauce. Béchamel Sauce may serve as the basis for many dishes. (See *French Cookery, Mornay Sauce, Sauce, Velouté Sauce, White Sauce* for additional information.)

Béchamel Sauce

> 2 tablespoons butter or margarine
> ¼ cup finely chopped onion
> 2 tablespoons all-purpose flour
> 1½ cups milk

Melt butter in saucepan. Add onion; cook till soft. Blend in flour and ¼ teaspoon salt. Add milk all at once. Cook quickly, stirring constantly, till mixture thickens. Makes 1½ cups.

BEEF

How to buy, store, and prepare both luxury and economy cuts of beef.

Beef is a full-grown ox, cow, bull, or steer, or the meat from these animals. Because of its appealing texture, flavor, and excellent nutritional value, beef has become the most popular meat in America.

This popularity is by no means a recent development. Early in history, man discovered the value of beef and successfully domesticated the animals. Since that time, beef has played an active role in the development of civilization.

Beef animals were probably man's first reliable source of food. After taming these animals, he no longer had to roam in search of meat, but could settle in one location. Drawings on cave walls of giant aurochs, ancestors of today's oxen, were left by early man as testimonies of beef's influence in their lives.

As civilization progressed, beef continued to play an active role. Culture and religion were influenced by beef. Artistic Egyptians painted scenes in tombs of busy market places where this meat was sold.

The people of the ancient Cretan, Greek, Roman, and Egyptian civilizations worshiped gods in the form of cows and bulls. One such idol was the golden calf made by the Israelites during their flight from Egypt. Today, certain cultures in India continue to worship cattle.

Beef, in one form or another, has had a remarkable influence on many emerging nations. The first cattle on the American continent were brought by the Spanish ex-

plorer, Hernando Cortés. Early in the sixteenth century, he introduced them in Mexico and from there they were taken into what is now the southwestern United States. These were added to in the following century, by the English who brought several varieties of beef to the American colonies, thus establishing the many strains which are in evidence today.

But this should not suggest that beef has always been abundant in America. In early colonial days, there was only one cow to every six families.

Today, three hundred years later, estimates show that over 100 pounds of beef are consumed each year by the average American—approximately 60 percent of his total meat diet.

Nutritional value: Beef, like most meats, is an excellent source of high-quality protein. It also contains some iron and the B vitamins, niacin and riboflavin.

Forms of beef

Modern supermarkets carry a wide array of beef and beef products. The consumer can select fresh, cured, freeze-dried, or canned or frozen beef to serve in menus. In the following discussion of each type, recipes are included to show how each might be used in a meal.

Fresh beef: This category includes the forms of beef sold from the refrigerated meat cases in markets. Fresh meats are processed and available to the consumer within six to ten days after slaughter. Cuts, labeled "aged," have had additional time in the cooler to make them more tender and to produce a characteristic "gamy" flavor. This processing increases the price.

Beef Pot Roast makes a full meal

← Cooked in 30 minutes with a pressure saucepan, Individual Pot Roasts develop the wonderful flavor of long, slow braising.

The vast selection of fresh meat on the market includes roasts, steaks, ribs, ground meats, variety cuts, and sausages.

Many of these cuts need only simple preparation to produce tasty, tender fare. The following recipe illustrates how easily fresh meat can be cooked.

Standing Rib Roast

Place standing rib roast, fat side up, in shallow roasting pan. Season with salt and pepper. Insert meat thermometer into center of roast; roast, uncovered, according to Beef Roasting Chart. Serves 2 or 3 per pound.

Some fresh beef is treated before cooking to increase tenderness. This can be done commercially or in the home.

Besides aging, there are two commercial processes used to tenderize beef. One involves a fruit enzyme, such as papain, which increases tenderness of meat during cooking. Cuts are marketed as pre-tendered beef. The other method uses machines to score the surface of the meat. This cuts and breaks the connective tissue and muscle fiber, thus tenderizing the meat. This beef is minute, cube, or sandwich steaks.

Minute Steak Sukiyaki

     4 minute steaks
     2 tablespoons salad oil
     1 10¾-ounce can beef gravy
     2 tablespoons soy sauce
     ½ pound fresh spinach
     1½ cups bias-cut celery slices
     ¼ cup bias-cut green onion slices
     1 6-ounce can chopped mushrooms
       Hot cooked rice

Cut minute steaks in strips; brown quickly in hot salad oil in skillet. Stir in gravy and soy sauce. Remove stems from spinach and drain mushrooms. Add spinach, mushrooms, celery, and onion to steak. Cook, stirring gently, 5 to 7 minutes or till vegetables are crisp-tender.

Serve meat and vegetable mixture over hot cooked rice. Pass additional soy sauce at serving time, if desired. Makes 4 servings.

1. *Standing Rib Roast* contains the rib bones, backbone, the rib eye muscle, and sometimes the cap muscle. *Rib Eye Roast*, also called a Delmonico Roast, is boneless and has the rib eye muscle. *Rolled Rib Roast* is a boneless, rolled, and tied Standing Rib Roast. Each of these may be roasted.

2. *Boneless Chuck Pot Roast*, boned, rolled, and tied, has fat interspersed between the muscle. *Blade Pot Roast* is identified by the blade bone, sometimes called a 7-bone. *Arm Pot Roast* has a round arm bone and may contain a cross section of rib bones. Braise these flavorful pot roasts.

3. *Flank Steak* is a boneless cut with many long muscle fibers and little fat. *Rolled Flank Steak* is often stuffed. *Flank Steak Fillets* (*pinwheels*) are cut from Rolled Flank Steak. A cube of suet is in the center for flavor and juiciness. Broil high-quality cuts, otherwise braise these cuts.

4. *Sirloin Tip Roast*, cut from the leg and sirloin, usually has the bone removed. Oval-shaped *Round Steak* is identified by the round bone. *Bottom Round Steak* often has both the bottom muscle and the *Eye of the Round*, a small egg-shaped muscle. *Top Round Steak* has the largest muscle. Roast or panfry high quality, otherwise braise.

5. *Corned Beef Brisket* is boneless and the surface fat is removed. Then the cut is cured. Cook in liquid. *Crosscut Shanks*, 1 to 1½ inches thick, have a round shank bone. Braise or cook in liquid for soup. *Short Ribs* contain a cross section of rib bone and have alternating layers of fat and lean. Braise or cook short ribs in liquid.

6. *Standing Rump Roast* is a triangular cut which contains the pelvic bone and may contain a portion of the backbone. *Rolled Rump Roast* is a boned, rolled, and tied Standing Rump Roast. Fat covers the roast and is interspersed in the many muscle layers. Roast high quality, otherwise braise.

1. *Rib Roast: Standing*, upper left, *Rib Eye*, lower left, *Rolled*, upper right.

2. *Pot Roast: Boneless Chuck*, upper left, *Blade*, lower left, *Arm*, right.

3. *Flank Steak*, left; *Rolled Flank Steak*, right; *Flank Steak Fillets*, bottom.

4. *Sirloin Tip Roast*, top; *Round Steak: Bottom and Eye*, middle, *Top*, right.

5. *Corned Beef Brisket*, upper left; *Crosscut Shanks*, lower left; *Short Ribs*, right.

6. *Standing Rump Roast*, lower left; *Rolled Rump Roast*, upper right.

Meats to be cooked can also be tenderized in the home. The homemaker can pound a steak with a mallet or the edge of a plate to break the tissues. Treating with a dry or liquid tenderizer also produces more tender beef. Follow the package directions when applying the tenderizer.

Deviled Flank Rolls

1 1½-pound beef flank steak
  Meat tenderizer
1 2¼-ounce can deviled ham
⅓ cup catsup
1 tablespoon salad oil
1 teaspoon kitchen bouquet

Pound thick end of steak with mallet to flatten slightly. Use meat tenderizer following label directions. Spread deviled ham over surface of steak. Roll up steak from long side; skewer securely at 1-inch intervals. Cut the rolled meat into 1-inch slices.

Combine catsup, salad oil, and kitchen bouquet. Brush both sides of meat with sauce. Place on rack in broiler pan. Broil 4 inches from heat for 5 minutes; turn. Brush with sauce; broil 5 minutes. Serves 2 or 3.

Ground meat is one of the biggest selling forms of fresh beef: hamburger, ground beef, ground chuck, ground round, and ground sirloin. The ground chuck, round, and sirloin are the lowest in fat, and shrink less. Therefore, they are more expensive than hamburger and ground beef which can have up to 30 percent fat.

Apple-Beef Patties

1 pound ground beef
1 cup cooked long-grain rice
1 slightly beaten egg
1 teaspoon Worcestershire sauce
½ cup water
1 teaspoon salt
½ 5-ounce jar spiced apple rings
    (5 rings)
¼ cup corn syrup
1 tablespoon lemon juice
2 teaspoons cornstarch

Combine beef, rice, egg, Worcestershire sauce, water, and salt. Shape into 5 thick patties; place in shallow baking pan. Drain 5 apple rings, reserving ½ cup syrup. Press 1 ring onto each patty. Bake uncovered at 350° for 35 minutes. Combine reserved apple syrup, corn syrup, and lemon juice in saucepan. Stir 2 teaspoons cold water into cornstarch; add to syrup mixture. Cook and stir till thickened and bubbly; spoon syrup mixture onto meat. Bake 5 minutes. Makes 5 servings.

Commercially ground beef is used in making sausage. This includes frankfurters, bologna, salami, and some cold cuts. These are made either entirely or partially with beef. Meat for the kosher market is an excellent example of the all-beef form.

Ten-in-One Sandwich Loaf

Bake one big, loaf sandwich and divide into 10 individual servings—

2 cups shredded process American
    cheese *or* 2 5-ounce jars process cheese spread
¼ cup mayonnaise or salad
    dressing
1 teaspoon prepared mustard
1 teaspoon grated onion
⅔ cup chopped ripe olives
    • • •
1 unsliced loaf white sandwich
    bread, about 11 inches long
20 thin slices salami (about
    ½ pound)
  Melted butter or margarine

Blend cheese, mayonnaise, mustard, and onion; stir in olives. Cut crusts from *top* and both sides of loaf. Make ½-inch slices, *cutting to, but not through,* bottom crust. Spread facing sides of first cut with cheese filling. Repeat with *every other* cut to make sandwiches.

Insert 2 salami slices in each "cheese sandwich." Spread remaining cheese over top. To hold shape, tie string around loaf 1 inch from top. Brush sides with butter.

Toast on baking sheet at 350° for 25 to 30 minutes. To serve, snip string and cut through bottom crust in unfilled sections.

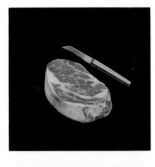
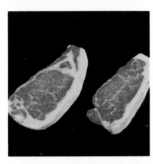
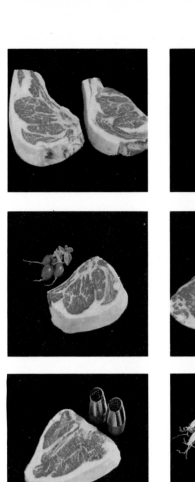
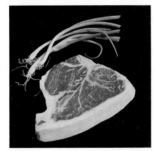
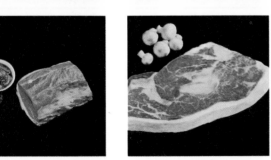
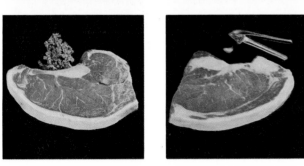

Rib Steak (left) identified by the rib bone, is cut from the rib section of the loin. It is tender and has well-developed flavor.

Rib Eye Steak (right) also called a Delmonico Steak, is a boneless cut from the eye of the beef rib. It has a well-developed flavor and is exceedingly tender.

Club Steak (left) is cut from the center loin and may contain the thirteenth rib. The large muscle is the loin eye; there is no tenderloin. Good for individual servings.

Top Loin Steak (right) also called New York or Kansas City, has only the loin eye muscle. Strip Steak (left) has the finger of the T-bone. Both are tender and flavorful.

T-Bone Steak (left) contains the loin and the tenderloin (the smaller muscle) separated by the finger of the T-bone.

Porterhouse Steak (right), considered by many to be the best steak, is cut from the center loin. The tenderloin muscle is larger than in a T-bone steak.

Chateaubriand (left) is the center cut from the tenderloin which has been removed from one side of the T-bone. It's a dining-out classic, listed on menus for "two or more."

Rib Bone Sirloin Steak (right) is the first steak cut from the sirloin section of the loin. It has a pin-shaped bone. These large steaks are good for serving several persons.

Flat Bone Sirloin Steak (left) is cut from the middle of the sirloin section. It can be identified by the flat-shaped bone.

Wedge Bone Sirloin (right) is cut from the sirloin section closest to the leg. The wedge-shaped bone is the identifying bone.

The category of fresh beef known as variety meats consists of cuts which are economical and highly nutritious. The brains, heart, kidney, liver, tripe (the plain or honey-combed lining of the stomach), marrow bone, sweetbread (the thymus glands of a young animal), and oxtail (the beef tail) are examples of variety beef cuts available at the meat counter.

Tripe and Onions

1½ pounds tripe
¼ cup butter or margarine
½ cup chopped onion
3 tablespoons all-purpose flour
1 teaspoon salt
⅛ teaspoon pepper
    Dash ground nutmeg
1 cup chicken broth
1 cup milk
    Toast points
    Paprika

In saucepan add water to tripe to cover. Cook tripe covered over low heat about 3 hours or till cut surface of tripe has clear, jellylike appearance. Drain and dice.

Melt butter in medium saucepan; add onion and cook till tender but not brown. Blend in flour, salt, pepper, and nutmeg. Add chicken broth and milk all at once. Cook and stir over medium-high heat till mixture is thick and bubbly. Add tripe; heat through.

Serve over toast points. Sprinkle with paprika. Makes 4 servings.

Cured Beef: In the days before refrigeration, curing was used to preserve meats. Now, however, the curing process is used because people enjoy the flavor of various cuts of cured beef. Since it is perishable, be sure to refrigerate cured beef products.

A popular type of cured beef, corned beef, is a brine-cured brisket or rump roast. Other types, also known as dried and chipped beef, are usually prepared from the round. These cuts are first cured in a pickling solution of salt and sugar or molasses. Then they are smoked and dried. Beef tongue and some sausages are additional examples of cured beef.

Corned Beef Dinner

1 3- to 4-pound corned beef
    brisket
½ cup chopped onion
2 cloves garlic, minced
2 whole bay leaves
        •   •   •
6 medium potatoes, peeled
6 small carrots, peeled
6 cabbage wedges
        •   •   •
    Prepared mustard
¼ cup brown sugar
    Dash ground cloves

Place corned beef in Dutch oven and barely cover with hot water. Add onion, garlic, and bay leaves. Cover; simmer 3 to 4 hours or till tender. Remove meat from liquid; keep warm.

Add potatoes and carrots to liquid in Dutch oven; cover and bring to boiling. Cook 10 minutes. Add cabbage and cook 20 minutes longer.

Meanwhile, glaze meat. Spread fat side of meat lightly with mustard. Combine brown sugar and cloves; sprinkle over mustard. Bake in shallow pan at 350° for 15 to 20 minutes. Arrange corned beef and vegetables on warm platter for serving. Makes 6 servings.

Freeze-dried beef: The newest form of beef on the market is freeze-dried. This porous, brittle beef has approximately the same volume as the fresh meat, yet it weighs much less. One pound of beef steak, for example, weighs four ounces freeze-dried.

To obtain this product, the manufacturer freezes the beef and evaporates the water. Freeze-dried products are then packed in airtight containers or vacuum packages that can be stored on the shelf at room temperature. The normal weight and texture are easily restored by adding a specified amount of water.

Because of the light weight and convenient storage, freeze-dried beef is used in space flights, by sportsmen on camping or hunting trips, and by manufacturers in packaged dry mixes.

Freeze-dried steaks and patties are among the products being introduced to the consumer in markets. These may be found in a supermarket or in a sports shop.

Corned Beef Dinner for family or company fare combines potatoes, carrots, and cabbage with a glazed corned beef brisket. Carve corned beef from two directions going across grain.

Canned, frozen, and packaged beef: Grocer's shelves carry a wide selection of canned, frozen and packaged beef products. Some of these are beef entrées, others contain beef in combination with sauces or vegetables, and a few are complete meals. Typical examples are roast beef, corned beef, baby foods, beef with gravy, beef with barbecue sauce, hash, stew, roast beef dinner, and spaghetti with meatballs.

These products have the advantages of easy storage and minimum preparation. Cans and packages can be kept on the cabinet shelf about a year. Frozen beef can be kept in the freezer several months.

Preparation of these beef products is usually simple and brief. They are heated or cooked according to package directions. Some can be cooked and served right from containers in which they were purchased.

Double-Beef Sandwiches

    12 slices rye bread
        Leaf lettuce
     4 ounces dried beef, pulled apart
     4 ounces sliced brick cheese
     4 ounces canned *or* cooked corned
        beef, thinly sliced
     2 large dill pickles, thinly sliced
     1 medium onion, thinly sliced
        Prepared horseradish

Spread 6 bread slices with butter and mustard; add layers of lettuce and dried beef. Spread with mayonnaise. Top each with a slice of cheese, corned beef, pickle, and onion. Top with more lettuce. Spread remaining bread lightly with horseradish and place atop lettuce.

Anchor each sandwich with wooden picks topped with a ripe olive, if desired. Serves 6.

How to select

Three guides help the consumer in selecting cuts of beef. These are the federal meat inspection stamp, the grade or packers brand, and the appearance of the meat.

The federal inspection stamp is put on beef which comes from healthy animals processed under sanitary conditions and labeled correctly and is required for all meat crossing state lines. The words "US INS'D & P'S'D" (US Inspected and Passed) and the number of the meat-packing plant appear on this round, purple stamp.

Federal grades, as differentiated from the inspection stamp, measure the quality of the meat. These grades, standard throughout the nation, are designated by the Meat Inspection Division of the U.S. Department of Agriculture. Grading is optional and is paid for by the meat packer.

A packer may elect to use his own grading system. Therefore, the consumer should become familiar with both the packers' grades and the federal grades.

Federally-graded beef carcasses are marked with shield-shaped stamps. Most cuts will bear part or all of a shield after the carcass is divided. This purple stamp is made with an edible vegetable compound and has the letters "USDA" and the name of the grade.

Prime is the top federal grade. The beef usually comes from young, well-fed cattle. Marbling, *liberal quantities of fat interspersed with the lean,* gives juiciness, tenderness, and flavor to the meat. This meat is frequently sold to hotels and restaurants.

Choice is high-quality beef with less fat than Prime. This meat, tender and juicy with a well-developed flavor, is one of the most popular with consumers.

Good has little fat therefore is not quite as juicy as the two higher grades. This quality is often purchased by the thrifty consumer who prefers more lean.

Standard has a very thin covering of fat and lacks juiciness. However, the mild-flavored meat is relatively tender when properly prepared. This grade appeals to

Cut	Approximate Weight (Pounds)	Internal Temp. on Removal from Oven	Approximate Cooking Time (Total Time)
BEEF ROASTING CHART			
Roast meat at constant oven temperature of 325° unless otherwise indicated.			
Standing Rib	4 to 6	140° (rare) / 160° (medium) / 170° (well done)	2¼ to 2¾ hrs. / 2¾ to 3¼ hrs. / 3¼ to 3½ hrs.
Standing Rib	6 to 8	140° (rare) / 160° (medium) / 170° (well done)	2¾ to 3 hrs. / 3 to 3½ hrs. / 3¾ to 4 hrs.
Rolled Rib	5 to 7	140° (rare) / 160° (medium) / 170° (well done)	3¼ to 3½ hrs. / 3¾ to 4 hrs. / 4½ to 4¾ hrs.
Rolled Rump	4 to 6	150° to 170°	2 to 2½ hrs.
Sirloin Tip	3½ to 4	150° to 170°	2 to 2¾ hrs.
Rib Eye or Delmonico (Roast at 350°)	4 to 6	140° (rare) / 160° (medium) / 170° (well done)	1½ to 1¾ hrs. / 1¾ hrs. / 2 hrs.
Tenderloin, whole (Roast at 425°)	4 to 6	140° (rare)	45 min. to 1 hr.
Tenderloin, half (Roast at 425°)	2 to 3	140° (rare)	45 to 50 min.

consumers who want a higher proportion of lean to fat or more servings per pound.

Commercial grade beef comes from older cattle and lacks tenderness. Long, slow cooking with moist heat is necessary to make it more chewable and to develop a rich, full flavor of the older beef.

Utility, Cutter, and Canner grades of meat are rarely found on the retail market. This meat comes from beef of varying ages and lacks tenderness. Its principal use is in ground beef, canned meats, and processed meat products such as bologna.

Appearance of the beef is another guide to selection. Look for meat with uniformly bright color, light-to-deep red, fine-grained texture, and firm, dry, well-marbled lean. The beef fat color, which is no longer used as a basis for grading, depends on the type feed given to the animal and does not indicate quality of the meat.

The bone can also reflect beef quality. Red, porous bones indicate the meat comes from a younger animal, therefore not as much marbling is needed for the meat to be tender. Bones become less red and harder as the animal matures and the meat should have more marbling to assure it will be juicy and tender.

The individual price is not a good guide to quality. Price is influenced by the amount of processing or handling and by the demand for the cut. For example, tender steaks are in greatest demand during the warm months when they are used for outdoor and quick cooking. During colder months, roasts are especially popular.

How much to buy: Approximately four ounces of uncooked, boneless beef should be purchased for each serving. This will allow for shrinkage during cooking and give the average three-ounce serving of meat planned for a meal.

A guide for the number of servings one pound of raw beef will yield is as follows: ground beef—4 servings, roast (bone-in)—2½ to 3 servings, roast (boneless)—3 to 3½ servings, short ribs—1½ servings, steak (bone-in)—2 to 3 servings, and steak (boneless)—3 to 4 servings.

The servings a pound of beef yields will vary with the amount of waste (fat and bone) which is on the meat. The appetites of the group served and the amount of other foods combined with the meat, such as stew vegetables and side dishes, will also have an influence on the number of servings in each pound.

How to store

Beef can be kept the maximum length of time without losing quality if stored properly. The most desirable refrigerator storage is a temperature of 35° to 40° with dry circulating air. Refrigerators usually have a shelf or drawer designed especially for this purpose. If there is no such area, then place the meat in a very cold section of the refrigerator, but not in the area that would freeze the meat.

Fresh beef should be loosely wrapped for refrigeration. Beef purchased in a prepackaged wrap can be stored unopened for one or two days. The package should be opened at both ends so air circulates for longer storage in the refrigerator.

This prepackaging is not sufficient for freezing. Beef should be securely wrapped in moisture-vaporproof paper or plastic before freezing, and stored at 0° F.

Frozen beef can be thawed before cooking or cooked in the frozen state. Leave the meat in the original wrap and thaw at room temperature or in the refrigerator. Cook soon after thawing. When cooking frozen beef, increase the cooking time or lower the cooking temperature. Frozen roasts demand one-and-a-half times longer than thawed roasts. Frozen steaks and chops take a lower broiling temperature.

Maximum Time for Beef Storage		
Beef Cut	Refrigerator	Freezer
Cold Cuts	3 to 5 days	Do not freeze
Cured	7 days	Do not freeze
Dried	10 to 12 days	Do not freeze
Ground	1 to 2 days	2 to 3 months
Roast	3 to 5 days	8 to 12 months
Steak	3 to 5 days	8 to 12 months
Stew	1 to 2 days	2 to 3 months
Variety	1 to 2 days	3 to 4 months
Cooked	1 to 2 days	2 to 3 months

How to prepare

Beef should be cooked at low to moderate temperatures. This gives maximum tenderness and juiciness and prevents evaporation, shrinkage, and dripping loss. To have the tastiest meat, use the proper cooking method for each cut.

Moist-heat cookery: This method involves cooking beef with added moisture, such as water, gravy, and stock, or in a covered utensil which keeps the moisture in the food from escaping. Moist-heat cookery improves less tender cuts by softening connective tissue. Braising and stewing are methods of moist-heat cookery.

Polynesian Pot Roast

    1 3-pound beef pot roast
    2 tablespoons salad oil
      Salt
    ¼ cup flaked coconut
    ¼ cup pineapple-apricot preserves
    1 tablespoon vinegar
    1 tablespoon soy sauce
    ½ teaspoon ground ginger
    ½ teaspoon grated lemon peel
      Dash pepper
    ¼ cup water
        •   •   •
    4 teaspoons cornstarch
    2 tablespoons water
      Pineapple rings
      Watercress *or* parsley
      Hot cooked rice

In large skillet or Dutch oven brown pot roast slowly in the 2 tablespoons salad oil. Sprinkle meat with a little salt. Combine flaked coconut, pineapple-apricot preserves, vinegar, soy sauce, ginger, lemon peel, pepper, and ¼ cup water; pour over meat. Cover skillet tightly; simmer meat till tender, about 2 to 2¼ hours.

Remove meat to heated platter. Skim fat from pan juices. Use about 1 cup of pan juices. Blend together cornstarch and 2 tablespoons cold water; add to pan juices. Cook and stir till thickened and bubbly. Spoon some sauce over meat; pass remainder. Garnish meat with pineapple rings and watercress or parsley. Serve with hot cooked rice. Makes 6 to 8 servings.

Individual Pot Roasts

    1 tablespoon shortening
    4 6-ounce pieces boneless beef
        chuck (1½ pounds)
      Salt
      Pepper
    ½ cup water
    4 carrots, peeled
    2 medium onions, quartered
    ½ cup cold water
    2 tablespoons all-purpose flour
    1 teaspoon liquid beef-flavored
        gravy base
        •   •   •
    8 ounces medium noodles, cooked
      Snipped parsley
      Paprika

Set heat selector of 4-quart electric pressure pan at 400° and heat shortening; brown meat well on all sides. Turn heat selector to "off." Season meat with salt and pepper.

Add first ½ cup water to electric pressure pan. (*Or* add 1 cup water if using a 6-quart electric pressure pan.)

*Close cover securely. Place pressure regulator on vent pipe and set heat selector at 425°. When pressure regulator attains a steady, gently rocking motion, turn heat selector to left till indicator light goes out. Cook 12 minutes. Turn heat selector to "off" and disconnect cord. Let pressure go down normally. After pressure has been completely reduced, remove pressure regulator and cover. Add carrots and onions. Repeat process beginning at *, cooking 5 minutes instead of 12 minutes. Remove meat and vegetables to heated platter.

For gravy, blend remaining ½ cup water with the 2 tablespoons flour. Stir into drippings in pan along with gravy base. Cook, stirring constantly, till thickened and bubbly. Cook, 2 to 3 minutes longer. Serve the individual roasts with gravy on bed of hot noodles. Garnish with snipped parsley; sprinkle with paprika. Makes 4 servings.

Grilled in- or out-of-doors

Marinate Lemon-Barbecued Chuck Steak→ in well-seasoned lemon juice for an economical steak that is flavorful, juicy, and tender.

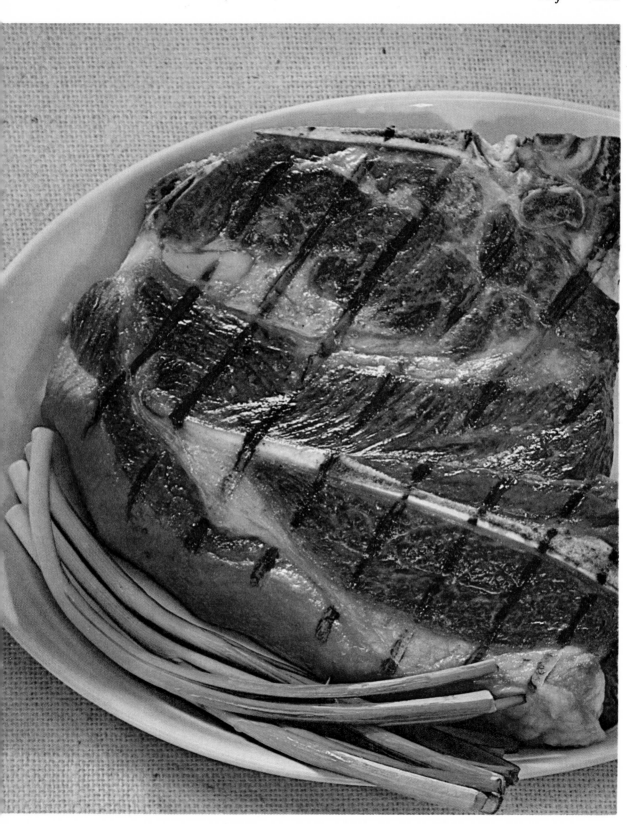

Beef with Dumplings

   1 3- to 4-pound beef pot roast
   2 tablespoons shortening
   1 16-ounce can tomatoes
  1/4 cup wine vinegar
   1 clove garlic, minced
   1 teaspoon salt
  1/2 teaspoon mixed pickling spices
  1/4 teaspoon pepper
   1 tube refrigerated biscuits
     (10 biscuits)
   1 tablespoon snipped parsley
  1/4 cup all-purpose flour
    Salt
    Pepper

Trim excess fat from roast. In Dutch oven or large skillet slowly brown meat on all sides in hot shortening. Add tomatoes, vinegar, 1/4 cup water, garlic, the 1 teaspoon salt, pickling spices, and 1/4 teaspoon pepper. Cover; cook slowly 2 1/2 hours or till meat is tender.

Place biscuits atop meat; sprinkle with parsley. Cover tightly and steam 15 minutes or till "dumplings" are done. Remove meat and dumplings to warm platter.

Skim most of fat from pan juices. Add water to juices to make 2 1/2 cups liquid. Put 1/2 cup cold water in screw-top jar. Add flour; cover and shake well till completely blended. Stir into juices; cook, stirring constantly, till gravy is thickened and bubbly. Season to taste with salt and pepper. Simmer 2 to 3 minutes, stirring occasionally. Serve pot roast gravy with meat and dumplings. Makes 6 to 8 servings.

Steak and Onions

   1 1 1/2- to 2-pound beef round steak,
     cut in serving-size pieces
   2 tablespoons shortening
   1 10 1/2-ounce can condensed cream
     of mushroom soup
   1 3 1/2-ounce jar undrained cock-
     tail onions
   1 tablespoon snipped parsley

In skillet brown meat slowly on both sides in hot shortening. Drain off excess fat. Combine soup, 1/4 cup water, and onions; pour over meat. Simmer covered for 1 1/2 hours or till tender. Sprinkle with parsley. Makes 6 servings.

Oven Beef Stew

Bakes in the oven for an easy meal—

   1 tablespoon all-purpose flour
  3/4 teaspoon salt
    Dash pepper
1 3/4 pound beef chuck, cut in
     1-inch cubes
   1 tablespoon shortening
       • • •
   1 10 1/2-ounce can condensed tomato
     soup
   1 soup can water (1 1/4 cups)
  3/4 cup chopped onion
  1/4 teaspoon dried basil leaves,
     crushed
       • • •
   2 medium potatoes, peeled and
     cubed
   2 medium carrots, cut in 1-inch
     pieces
  1/4 cup dry red wine *or* water

Combine flour, salt, and pepper; coat meat cubes in seasoned flour. Brown in hot shortening in small Dutch oven; add soup, water, onion, and basil. Cover and bake at 375° about 1 hour. Add potatoes, carrots, and wine or water. Cover and bake 1 hour longer or till tender. Makes 2 or 3 servings.

Dry-heat cookery: This process involves cooking without the addition of moisture. Broil, panbroil, panfry, and roasts are all classified as dry heat cooking methods.

Only tender cuts of beef should be cooked in this way since this process does not have the long, slow cooking with moisture which helps to tenderize meat.

Beef Rib Supreme

Have meatman cut one 4- to 6-pound roast as for Delmonico or rib eye roast, but with 3-inch-length ribs still attached. Place roast, fat side up, on rack in shallow roasting pan. Insert meat thermometer. Roast uncovered according to Beef Roasting Chart. To serve trim with cherry tomatoes and sprigs of parsley or watercress, if desired. Allow 2 or 3 servings for each pound of meat.

Lemon-Barbecued Chuck Steak

   1 4-pound chuck steak, 1½ inches
     thick
   1 teaspoon grated lemon peel
  ⅔ cup lemon juice
  ⅓ cup salad oil
   2 teaspoons monosodium glutamate
 1½ teaspoons salt
  ⅛ teaspoon pepper
   1 teaspoon Worcestershire sauce
   1 teaspoon prepared mustard
   2 green onion tops, sliced

Score fat edges of meat. Place in shallow dish. Combine remaining ingredients; pour over steak. Let stand 3 hours at room temperature or 6 hours in refrigerator, turning steak several times while it is marinating.

Remove steak from marinade; with paper toweling, remove excess moisture. Cook over hot coals or broil about 12 minutes for rare or 15 minutes for medium, brushing occasionally with marinade. Carve meat across grain in thin slices. Makes 6 to 8 servings.

Roast Beef Tenderloin

Remove surface fat and connective tissue from one 4- to 6-pound whole beef tenderloin. Place on rack in shallow roasting pan; season to taste with salt and pepper. Tuck small end under. Insert meat thermometer in thickest part.

Brush meat with salad oil. Roast uncovered according to Beef Roasting Chart. Makes 2 or 3 servings per pound.

Stuffed Tenderloin

   1 3-pound beef tenderloin
  ½ cup chopped onion
  ½ cup chopped celery
   6 tablespoons butter or margarine
   3 cups soft bread crumbs
   1 6-ounce can sliced mushrooms,
     drained
    Salt
    Pepper
   3 slices bacon

Split and slightly flatten tenderloin with mallet. In skillet cook onion and celery with butter.

Stir in bread crumbs and mushrooms; spread mixture over *half* the meat. Bring second side of meat over; fasten edges with skewers. Season with salt and pepper; place bacon slices across top of meat.

Roast uncovered in shallow pan at 325° for about 1¼ hours till rare or medium-rare as desired. Makes 6 to 8 servings.

How to serve

Beef is served primarily as a main dish. However, it can be served at other courses for an exciting variation to the menu. Beef makes hearty appetizers, serves as a foundation for tossed or molded salads, flavors beverages such as hot bouillon, and provides filling, nutritious snacks.

Whether served quite simply or very elaborately, beef is the core of the average American's diet. (See also *Meat*.)

Dilly Beef Cartwheel

   1 cup dairy sour cream
   4 teaspoons *dry* onion soup mix
   1 tablespoon prepared horseradish
    Dash freshly ground pepper
   4 slices large round rye bread
 1½ cups shredded lettuce
 1½ cups shredded endive *or* spinach
   1 medium tomato, sliced
   6 thin slices cooked roast beef
   6 dill pickle strips
   1 medium tomato, cut in wedges
    Milk
    Pitted ripe olives

Combine sour cream, onion soup mix, horseradish, and pepper. Arrange *2 slices* of the bread, bottom to bottom, to form large circle; spread with a *third* of the sour cream mixture.

Toss together lettuce and endive; place *two-thirds* atop bread. Top with tomato slices. Place remaining bread atop lettuce mixture; spread with *half* of remaining sour cream mixture. Top with remaining lettuce mixture.

Make 6 cornucopias of beef with pickle in center of each; arrange with tomato wedges atop sandwich. Thin remaining sour cream mixture with a little milk; drizzle over sandwich. Garnish completed cartwheel with olives. Cut in wedges to serve. Makes 6 servings.

Oriental Skillet Supper

½ cup green pepper strips
⅓ cup bias-cut celery
1 tablespoon salad oil
1 large *or* 2 small minute steaks,
    cut in ¼-inch strips
⅓ cup cold water
1 tablespoon soy sauce
2 teaspoons cornstarch
½ teaspoon sugar
¼ teaspoon salt
1 medium tomato, peeled and
    cut in wedges
1 cup hot cooked rice
¼ teaspoon ground ginger

In heavy skillet cook green pepper and celery in salad oil till crisp-tender. Remove and set aside. Add meat to hot skillet; brown quickly.

Combine water, soy sauce, cornstarch, sugar, and salt; add to skillet. Cook and stir till mixture is thickened and bubbly. Add celery, green pepper, and tomato; heat through. Serve over rice tossed with ginger. Pass additional soy sauce, if desired. Makes 2 servings.

Beef and Mushroom Salad

4 cups cooked beef cut in julienne
    strips
1 cup sliced fresh mushrooms
¼ cup thinly sliced green onions
½ cup mayonnaise *or* salad
    dressing
½ cup dairy sour cream
1 tablespoon milk
  Lettuce cups
  Paprika

Combine beef, mushrooms, and onion in large bowl. Blend together mayonnaise, sour cream, milk, ½ teaspoon salt, and dash pepper; toss with meat mixture. Chill. Serve in lettuce cups; sprinkle with paprika. Makes 5 or 6 servings.

Dinner for two

← Cooks fast, so set the table and begin cooking the rice before starting Oriental Skillet Supper. Quick to clean up, too.

Stuffed Hamburger Roll

¼ cup chopped onion
2½ cups ¼-inch bread cubes,
    toasted (about 4 slices)
    •   •   •
1½ pounds ground beef
1 egg
¼ teaspoon dried sage leaves,
    crushed
4 ounces sharp process American
    cheese, shredded (1 cup)

Combine onion and ⅓ cup water; simmer covered 5 minutes. Add bread cubes; toss. Combine beef, egg, sage, ½ teaspoon salt, and dash pepper. On waxed paper pat meat into 14x8-inch rectangle. Spread bread mixture over; sprinkle ¾ *cup* cheese over bread mixture.

Starting at narrow end, roll meat jelly-roll fashion. Place seam side down in 8½x4½x2½-inch loaf dish. Bake uncovered at 350° for 1 hour and 10 minutes. Top with remaining cheese; bake till melted. Makes 6 servings.

BEEF BACON—A misnomer for the meat from the belly of a beef animal. Government regulations forbid it being labeled "bacon" because it does not come from a hog. The correct name is "breakfast beef." It is cured and smoked like bacon but is darker in color. Cook it the same way as pork bacon. A half pound of breakfast beef will average from 12 to 14 slices.

BEEF EXTRACT—Beef stock which is reduced by boiling to a clear, soluble paste. Beef extract is one of the basic ingredients in commercial products such as beef-flavored soup and gravy bases. Beef extract itself can be used to flavor gravies, sauces, soups, vegetable, and meat dishes.

BEEF-FLAVORED BASE—A liquid, paste, or dry product used for making gravy, sauce, and broth or for flavoring meat dishes. The beef flavor usually comes from beef extract and artificial flavorings.

BEEF TEA—A hot beverage made by heating pieces of lean beef in water, then straining the liquid. Beef extract dissolved in hot water also makes beef tea.

BEEF WELLINGTON—Roasted fillet of beef, coated with *pâte de foie gras* or *duxelles*, wrapped in pastry, then baked.

BEER—An alcoholic beverage flavored with hops and obtained by the fermentation of malted cereals. It is either top or bottom fermented which determines its classification as ale, porter, stout, or lager.

Beer of one kind or another has been known to man for many centuries, either as a beverage or for use in religious ceremonies, though its exact historical date is not known. The earliest recorded date reaches back to 6,000 B.C. with Babylonian clay tablets. Sketches on these tablets indicate that these people used beer for sacrificial purposes. Beer was also used for religious purposes in the time of the Egyptian Pharaohs. The Egyptian goddess of motherhood, Isis, is credited with having introduced brewing, and Rameses III is recorded as having given over 400,000 jugs of beer to the deities.

In Medieval times this religious influence was still present. English monks developed brewing into a fine art. By the ninth century, most monasteries in England had a brewery, and large monasteries often had more than one brewery, each one producing a different kind of beer.

Besides using beer for sacrificial and religious purposes, the ancient Egyptians also regarded it as a medicine and as an important food item for the peasants, who were given daily four loaves of bread and two jugs of beer by the king. The slightly sourish beer given to the peasants usually contained the spent grain hulls so had to be chewed as well as drunk.

This early Egyptian beer was usually brewed from bread made of coarsely crushed, germinated barley. Pieces of this underbaked bread were soaked in water in a large jug until fermentation was started by wild airborne yeast. Fermentation was allowed to proceed for about a day, and then the mass was refined for warriors, priests, and kings by forcing it through a sieve. The foaming beverage obtained after sieving was ready to drink.

Beer production, in fact, is possible in any area where cereals are grown. Thus there is evidence that centuries ago it was brewed in China, South America, Rome, Greece, and Spain. Its introduction into northern European countries was probably brought about by the inability to grow grapes for wine in cold climates.

Brewing greatly interested Charlemagne, king of the Franks, and he became an authority on the brewing process. During his reign all brewmasters had to come to his court to receive instruction on the latest brewing methods. This was considered so important that brewmasters for Charlemagne's court were chosen with as much care as were court leaders.

This is not meant to suggest that beer was drunk for alcohol alone. The people of historical times often used beer as a substitute for water, which was often unfit for human consumption. The brewing of beer was one method of purification. Taking this view, young people were, and in many countries still are, allowed to drink the beverage, which was frequently of a fairly low alcoholic content.

The flavor of the beer of ancient and medieval times bore little resemblance to the beer of today. Although hops are now used to flavor beer, dates, honey, cinnamon, and herbs were commonly used until well into the fourteenth century when hops became universally available and favored.

Beer production in the Americas dates back to the Indians. In 1502, friendly Central American Indians presented Columbus with "a sort of wine made from maize, resembling English beer." Beer also had a part in the history of the pilgrims. In a manuscript dated 1622, one of the Pilgrim Fathers records that Plymouth was chosen as a landing site because "We could not now take time for further search or consideration; our victuals being much spent, especially our beer . . ."

By the time of the American Revolution, brewing had become an economically important industry in the colonies. Such Revolution leaders as Patrick Henry, Thomas Jefferson, and Samuel Adams, were interested in the brewing industry. Many of them were brewers. Recorded is a beer recipe written by George Washington.

Lager beer, a light-bodied, highly carbonated beer was introduced into the United States by German immigrants in the

1840s. The Germans established breweries in Cincinnati, Milwaukee, and St. Louis—those cities which have since become renowned brewing centers. They also introduced large beer gardens which soon became famous for their relaxed atmosphere, lively music, and good beer.

Since early colonial days, beer has provided revenue for the American government. In 1688, the Massachusetts Bay colony put the first tax on beer. This practice soon spread from state to state. However, during the Revolutionary War, most of the taxes on beer were dropped temporarily in an attempt to revive the flagging brewing industry by promoting the consumption of beer over distilled beverages.

A federal tax was imposed on imported beers by the First Congress. American-produced beers were not federally taxed until the Civil War when $1 was levied on each barrel. Today, beer is taxed by both federal and state governments.

Types of beer: Throughout the world, there are many types and kinds of beer, but generally they are divided by both fermenting process (top or bottom fermented) and color (light or dark).

Lager beer is bright, light-bodied, highly carbonated beer that is allowed to ferment until all the yeast has settled on the bottom of the fermentation vat. Lager is the German word for "to store" and originally lager beers were stored for several months to allow them to mellow and become carbonated. The term lager, however, is today applied to all beers brewed using bottom fermenting yeasts. Most beers produced in the United States are lagers.

Originally ale contained no hops and was drunk fresh. Today, however, ale is a light-colored beer brewed using a top fermenting yeast. Ale has a sharper taste than lager beer and a stronger hops flavor. Although relatively little ale is made or consumed in the United States, it continues to be the favorite type of beer in England.

Stout and porter are two common types of beer. While stout is a very dark, heavy, malt beer that is often slightly sweet and usually highly flavored with hops, porter is characterized by a very heavy, creamy foam. This latter type is usually lower in alcoholic content, and derives its name from the London porters who favored it over other types of beer.

Bock beer is a heavy, sweet beer traditionally sold for only a few weeks in the spring. The malt used in brewing this beer is highly caramelized by kiln-roasting it. This caramelization is responsible for the characteristic dark color of bock beer.

Beer also is characterized by its color, either light or dark. The color difference is due to the use of roasted malt and added burnt sugar to give the dark, rich color that distinguishes dark beer.

A light-bodied beer, Pilsner, originally was a beer brewed in Pilsen, Czechoslovakia. The pure water of this city gave the beer a clean, fresh flavor. Nowadays the term Pilsner is often used to describe any light-bodied lager beer.

Compared to wine and spirits, beer is a mildly alcoholic beverage. In the United States, the alcoholic content of beer ranges from 3 percent to 4.5 percent by weight with an average of 3.7 percent by weight.

A characteristic of beer is its ability to form a "head." A thick froth on the top of a freshly poured glass of beer is used as an indication of good quality.

How beer is produced: The brewing processes of this country can be divided into four main steps—making the wort, boiling and hopping the wort, fermenting the brew, and processing the beer.

The first step is mixing crushed barley malt plus cereals, usually corn or rice, with water at carefully controlled temperatures. As the sugar dissolves in the water, this sugar solution, known in the trade as wort, is drawn off into a large kettle. Rotating water sprinklers then spray the grain to make sure all the sugar is extracted from the barley malt, leaving only the empty grain husks as waste.

The next step is boiling the wort. During this boiling, the hops are added in several portions and the bitter hops flavor combines with the sweetness of the wort. At the completion of this boiling, the hops are strained out and the wort is cooled.

The alcohol in beer is produced during the third brewing step, fermentation. A special type of cultured yeast, capable of converting sugar into alcohol and carbon dioxide, is added to the cooled wort. Fermentation is then allowed to continue for several days until the yeast settles to the bottom with lager beer or rises to the top with ale, porter, and stout.

Although the brewing process is now complete, the beer must be further processed before it is sold. The beer is aged by storing it at or near freezing temperatures to mellow the flavor and aid in preserving stability and quality. It is then filtered, carbonated, put into bottles, cans, or kegs, and usually pasteurized. Pasteurization is employed to destroy any minute quantities of bacteria or other living microorganisms. If the beer was not pasteurized, these microorganisms might multiply and cause the beer to spoil. Canned or bottled draft beer is stored for only short periods of time so the microorganisms are removed by microfiltering rather than pasteurization.

Throughout the world, barley is the most widely used grain for malting. The barley malt, often called the most important brewing ingredient, is largely responsible for the characteristic beer flavor.

The distinctive flavor of many famous beers is attributed to the brewing water. Many breweries which were established near natural sources of water for convenience continue to operate at this site because it is considered that the water gives the beer a desirable flavor. Breweries using other water supplies often add minerals to the water to obtain the desired flavor.

How to use: As a beverage, beer is drunk both alone and with meals and it is popularly associated with all types of informal social activities. This association is recognized in the English phrase, "beer and skittles," originally referring to beer and a game of ten-pins but now used to describe any type of enjoyable activity.

Beer can also be used in cooking. Although the alcohol is driven off by the heat, beer is used in cooking to add the beer flavor to various dishes. This flavor is especially compatible with cheese, and beer is the traditional liquid used in Welsh Rabbit. Beer is also an ingredient in sauces, stews, pot roasts, other meat and seafood dishes, and meat marinades.

Beef Pot Roast in Beer

  1 3- to 4-pound beef rump roast
  2 tablespoons all-purpose flour
  2 tablespoons shortening
  1 teaspoon salt
    Dash pepper
½ cup beer
  2 bay leaves
        •   •   •
  6 small whole onions
  4 medium carrots, peeled and
      cut in 1-inch pieces
        •   •   •
    About 1 cup beer
½ cup cold water
¼ cup all-purpose flour
  2 tablespoons catsup

Coat beef roast on all sides with the 2 tablespoons flour. In Dutch oven or large skillet brown roast slowly on all sides in hot shortening. Season with salt and pepper. Add the ½ cup beer and bay leaves. Cover tightly; simmer 1½ hours. Remove bay leaves.

Add onions and carrots. Cook 1 hour or till meat and vegetables are tender. Remove to heated platter. Skim fat from meat juices. Add enough beer to juices to make 1½ cups.

Put cold water in shaker with ¼ cup all-purpose flour. Shake well. Stir into juices with catsup. Cook, stirring constantly till thickened and bubbly. Season. Cook and stir 2 to 3 minutes longer. Serve with meat and vegetables. Makes 6 to 8 servings.

Shrimp in Beer

  2 pounds raw shrimp in shells
  3 12-ounce cans beer
  2 dried red peppers
  1 bay leaf
    Dash dried thyme leaves,
      crushed

Put raw shrimp in a saucepan and cover with beer. Bring to boiling; add red peppers, bay leaf, and crushed thyme. Simmer, covered, for about 5 minutes, or till shrimp is bright pink. Cool in the cooking liquid.

Shell and devein shrimp; chill thoroughly. Arrange the shrimp in a chilled bowl and pierce each one with a cocktail skewer.

Beef Rarebit

Beef adds a new twist to rarebit—

  1 pound ground beef
  ½ cup chopped onion
  ¼ cup chopped green pepper
  ¾ cup beer
     Dash cayenne
 12 ounces sharp process American
     cheese, shredded (3 cups)

       • • •

  6 English muffins, split and
    toasted

In skillet brown meat with onion and green pepper; drain off excess fat. Add beer and cayenne. Stir in cheese; heat till melted. Serve over muffins. Makes 6 servings.

Beer-Sauced Burgers

Tangy beer sauce brushed over grilled beef patties. Great for an outdoor barbecue—

   2 tablespoons chopped onion
   2 tablespoons chopped green
      pepper
   2 tablespoons butter or
      margarine, melted
  ½ cup catsup
   2 teaspoons cornstarch
   1 teaspoon Worcestershire sauce
  ½ cup beer

       • • •

 1½ pounds ground beef
   1 teaspoon salt
   6 hamburger buns, split
     and toasted

In small saucepan cook onion and green pepper in butter or margarine till tender but not brown. Combine catsup, cornstarch, and Worcestershire sauce. Stir into vegetables in saucepan. Add beer. Heat, stirring constantly, till mixture just starts to boil.

Combine beef and salt. Shape into 6 patties, ½ inch thick. Brush with beer sauce and grill over *medium* coals 8 to 10 minutes. Turn and continue grilling for 6 to 8 minutes or till desired doneness; brush occasionally with sauce. Serve burgers in hamburger buns; spoon more hot beer sauce over. Makes 6 servings.

BEET—Any of a number of related plants which have edible leaves and a thick, fleshy, white, purplish red, or red taproot.

Originating wild in the Mediterranean area, beets spread eastward in prehistoric times. Only the leaves were eaten, however, until early in the Christian Era, when the fleshy red taproot of the beet was recognized as a tasty vegetable. Roman writings of the second and third centuries contain the first directions for cooking beet roots. It was included in Fourteenth century English recipes, and by 1800 had become popular in Europe. It is not known when beets came to America or which settlers introduced them, but the cultivation of one variety was recorded in 1806.

Today, beets are widely cultivated as a vegetable with California, Texas, New Jersey, Ohio, New York, and Colorado as the chief producers in the United States.

Nutritional value: Beet greens are an excellent source of vitamin A. One-half cup of cooked beet greens supplies all of the recommended daily allowance for this vitamin. The beet taproot makes a less significant contribution to the diet but does contain small amounts of thiamine, riboflavin, vitamin C, and vitamin A.

Beets are relatively low in calories with ½ cup of cooked beets yielding 27 calories while ½ cup of cooked beet greens adds only 18 calories to the day's count.

Types of beets: The four types of beets that are widely cultivated are the common garden beet, the sugar beet, swiss chard, and the mangel or mangel-wurzel.

The common garden beet is cultivated as a vegetable. Both the tender greens and bright red, turnip like taproot of the garden beet are commonly eaten.

Swiss chard is a vegetable grown for its edible leaves and served much like spinach. The mangel-wurzel is grown, especially in Europe, for cattle feed.

Beets are also raised commercially to produce sugar. The type of beet used has a high sugar content and forms the base for a major industry.

Other varieties of beets are grown in flower gardens for their ornamental red, green, or yellow foliage.

How to select: Fresh beets are available all year round but the peak season is from June to October. Look for rounded beets with a smooth, firm flesh. Medium-sized beets are less likely to be tough. Since the beet top deteriorates rapidly without immediately affecting the taproot quality, beets that have wilted leaves are not necessarily of inferior quality.

Spring beets are usually sold with the tender, young tops still intact. Select greens that are thin-ribbed, fresh, green, and not wilted or slimy. Very tiny beets attached to the greens are also desirable.

How to store: Store fresh beets in the vegetable crisper of the refrigerator. The late fall crop of beets are usually sold without leaves and can be stored for longer periods of time in a cool dry place.

The beet greens are highly perishable but can be washed and stored for a short time in a plastic bag in the refrigerator.

How to prepare: To hold the red color when cooking fresh beets, cut off all but one inch of the stem and root. Scrub thoroughly but do not peel. Cook covered in boiling salted water till tender. When partially cooled, the skins will slip off easily.

To cook beet greens, wash them thoroughly under cold running water. Do not cut off any tiny beets. Remove any poor leaves. Place the greens in a saucepan with a tight-fitting lid and salt lightly. Cover and cook without any water except that which clings to the leaves. Reduce the heat when steam begins to form. Cook until tender, turning frequently with fork.

How to use: Beets are a colorful addition to the menu. Serve cooked beets whole, sliced, diced, riced, mashed, or cut in julienne strips. For a change from plain buttered beets, season them with allspice, caraway seed, cloves, tarragon, ginger, mustard, bay leaves, chili powder, celery seed, dill, nutmeg, or thyme.

For a fancier menu, serve Harvard beets or beets with sour cream, dill sauce, lemon butter, or Béarnaise sauce. The Russian soup, *borsch,* is made with beets. Red flannel hash, a traditional New England dish, gets its red color from beets.

Orange-Glazed Beets

> 3 tablespoons butter
> ¼ cup orange marmalade
> 1 tablespoon orange juice
> 2 cups cooked *or* canned beets, drained

Melt butter in skillet; stir in orange marmalade and orange juice. Add beets. Cook and stir over low heat till beets are hot and glazed, about 6 to 8 minutes. Makes 4 servings.

Can-Can Borsch

> 1 10½-ounce can condensed beef broth, chilled
> 1 8- to 8½-ounce can julienne or diced beets, chilled (1 cup)
> 2 tablespoons lemon juice
> Dairy sour cream
> Snipped chives

Combine chilled beef broth, canned beets (with liquid), and lemon juice. Serve in chilled bowls. Top each serving with a large dollop of sour cream and a sprinkling of snipped chives. Makes 3 servings.

Cranberry-Orange Beets

> 1 cup cranberry-juice cocktail
> 1 tablespoon cornstarch
> 1 tablespoon sugar
> 2 16-ounce cans sliced beets, drained
> ¼ teaspoon grated orange peel

In saucepan gradually stir cranberry juice into cornstarch, sugar, and dash salt. Cook and stir over medium heat till mixture thickens and bubbles. Add beets and orange peel. Simmer, uncovered, 10 minutes. Serves 4.

Ruby red beets

Prime quality beets are smooth and rounded →
without any ridges or blemishes. For added nutrients, use the beet greens, also.

Bring out the best in Orange Glazed Beets with this easy-to-do glaze of orange marmalade, butter, and orange juice. Use this same glaze over Brussels sprouts. Top with orange twist.

Beets in Cream

> ¼ cup dairy sour cream
> 1 tablespoon vinegar
> 1 teaspoon finely chopped
>   green onion
> ¾ teaspoon sugar
> ½ teaspoon salt
>   Dash cayenne
> . . .
> 2½ cups halved cooked beets,
>   drained

Combine dairy sour cream, vinegar, chopped green onion, sugar, salt, and cayenne. Add sauce to beets. Heat slowly, stirring occasionally to coat beets evenly. (Do not boil.) Serve hot. Makes 4 or 5 servings.

Beet-Onion Medley

> 1 16-ounce can sliced
>   beets (2 cups)
> 2 tablespoons butter or margarine
> 1 cup thin onion slices
> ¼ cup chopped celery
> . . .
> 1 tablespoon snipped parsley

Drain the beets, *reserving 2 tablespoons juice.* In skillet or saucepan melt butter or margarine; add drained beets, the reserved 2 tablespoons juice, onion slices, and chopped celery.

Cover; cook over low heat till onion and celery are tender, about 12 minutes. Season with salt and pepper. Sprinkle with snipped parsley. Makes 4 servings.

Zippy Beet Salad

    1 envelope unflavored gelatin
       (1 tablespoon)
⅔ cup pickled-beet liquid
½ teaspoon salt
¼ teaspoon grated onion
      • • •
    1 cup chopped pickled beets
    1 cup finely shredded cabbage

In small saucepan soften unflavored gelatin in ½ cup cold water. Heat and stir over low heat till gelatin is dissolved.

    To pickled-beet liquid, add water to make 1½ cups; add to gelatin along with salt and grated onion. Chill till partially set. Fold in pickled beets and shredded cabbage. Turn into 3-cup mold; chill till firm. Unmold on a bed of greens. Makes 6 servings.

Pickled Beets

⅓ cup vinegar
¼ cup sugar
½ teaspoon ground cinnamon
¼ teaspoon salt
¼ teaspoon ground cloves
    2 cups sliced cooked beets

Combine ¼ cup water, vinegar, sugar, ground cinnamon, salt, and ground cloves. Heat to boiling; add sliced, cooked beets. Cover and simmer 5 minutes; chill.

Hawaiian Beets

    2 tablespoons brown sugar
    1 tablespoon cornstarch
¼ teaspoon salt
    1 8¾-ounce can pineapple tidbits
    1 tablespoon butter or margarine
    1 tablespoon lemon juice
    1 16-ounce can sliced beets,
       drained (2 cups)

In saucepan combine brown sugar, cornstarch, and salt. Stir in pineapple tidbits. Cook and stir till mixture thickens and bubbles. Add butter, lemon juice, and sliced beets. Cook over medium heat about 5 minutes, or till heated through. Makes 4 or 5 servings.

Potato-Beet Salad

Horseradish gives real zip to this potato salad—

    2 16-ounce cans sliced potatoes,
       drained (4 cups)
    1 16-ounce can cut green beans,
       drained (2 cups)
    1 8-ounce can tiny whole beets,
       drained and halved (1 cup)
½ cup sliced celery
½ cup sliced green onion
½ cup sliced radishes
    Salt
    Freshly ground pepper
½ to ¾ cup Horseradish
    Dressing

Thoroughly chill the sliced potatoes, green beans, and beets; toss with celery, onion, and radishes. Sprinkle with salt and pepper. Just before serving, toss with Horseradish Dressing. Makes 6 to 8 servings.

    Horseradish Dressing: Combine ½ cup mayonnaise or salad dressing, ¼ cup dairy sour cream, and 3 tablespoons prepared horseradish. Add 1 cup clear French-style salad dressing with spices and herbs; stir till smooth; chill. Makes 1¾ cups dressing.

Splash a touch of the islands to Hawaiian Beets with pineapple tidbits and glaze. Serve as an accompaniment for pork chops.

Raisin-Sauced Beets

      1 16-ounce can sliced beets
          (2 cups)
    ⅓ cup raisins
        •   •   •
    ¼ cup sugar
      1 teaspoon cornstarch
      3 tablespoons lemon juice
      2 tablespoons butter or margarine

Drain beets, *reserving ⅓ cup liquid.* In medium saucepan combine reserved beet liquid and raisins. Cover; simmer over low heat till raisins are plumped, about 5 minutes.

Combine sugar and cornstarch; stir into raisins in pan. Add lemon juice and butter or margarine; cook and stir over medium heat till slightly thickened. Stir in beets and simmer till mixture is heated through, about 5 minutes. If desired, garnish with a twist of lemon. Makes 4 servings.

Beet and Apple Skillet

    ½ cup chopped onion
    ¼ cup butter or margarine
        •   •   •
      6 medium beets, cooked and
          sliced *or* 1 16-ounce can
          sliced beets, drained
      2 medium apples, cored and
          chopped
    ½ teaspoon salt
        Dash ground nutmeg

In saucepan cook onion in butter till tender. Add beets and apples. Cover; cook slowly till apples are tender. Add salt and ground nutmeg. Makes 4 to 6 servings.

Beet greens are very nutritious and can be used fresh in salads or cooked and served as a vegetable similar to spinach.

A timesaving way to add ruby red beets to the menu is to make use of the canned products. Canned beets are available whole, sliced, diced, in julienne strips, or pickled. Bright-red pickled beets are a colorful, spicy accompaniment for roasted beef or pork, casseroles, and golden brown fried chicken. (See also *Vegetable.*)

BEIGNET *(bān yā)*—The French name for fritters of various types made with a rich yeast dough, cream puff paste, or batter and deep-fat fried. Some of the fillings commonly used are fruits, vegetables, sweet custard cream, meat, fish, poultry, cheese, nuts, and rice.

BELGIAN ENDIVE—A winter vegetable with fleshy leaves and a slightly bitter flavor that is grown from chicory roots. Belgian endive comes in smooth slender stalks that are white with a slight greenish tinge. In Belgium, this vegetable is also known as witloof or "white-leaf" chicory and in other parts of the world, it is known as French endive or chicory.

This vegetable was accidentally discovered in 1846. Botanists at the Brussels Botanical Gardens were trying to develop a coffee substitute from treated chicory roots. One of the gardeners involved in the project left one of these roots in his basement for several days. Upon returning, he was surprised to find that a number of delicate white leaves had sprouted from the treated chicory root.

Tests determined that these leaves were edible and cultivation of this tasty vegetable began. Cultivation has increased so much that it is now a Belgian specialty.

Whether it's called witloof, French endive, chicory, or Belgian endive, the smooth, slender stalks of this vegetable are tasty.

Although Belgian endive is harvested during the frost and snow of winter, production of this vegetable begins in the spring when chicory seeds are sown between rows of other vegetables. The plant is taken up before it flowers and its leaves removed for fodder. The chicory roots are then stored until fall when carefully selected specimens are cut down to lengths of nine inches, replanted in heated, roofed trenches, and covered with straw. In six weeks, the heads, which grow upright in an elongated stalk, have reached the harvesting length of six to seven inches.

This vegetable is favored by Belgian farmers because they are able to grow several crops during the growing season. And, since the seeds are planted first between rows of other vegetables and harvested after other crops, no additional acreage is necessary for their cultivation.

This biennial plant has a biological cycle comprised of a vegetative and a generative phase. During the first year of growth, the vegetative phase, the head used as a vegetable is produced. During the second year of growth, the generative phase, the flowers and seeds are produced.

Until a few years ago, all Belgian endives available in United States markets were imported from Europe. Now, however, local growers supply almost all of the vegetable used in this country.

Belgian Endive-Ham Rolls

An elegant entrée—

> 4 stalks Belgian endive
> 1/4 cup water
> 2 tablespoons lemon juice
> 1/2 teaspoon salt
>   Dash pepper
> 8 slices boiled ham
>   • • •
> 2 tablespoons butter or margarine
> 2 tablespoons all-purpose flour
> 1/2 cup milk
> 1/2 cup chicken broth
> 4 ounces sharp process American
>   cheese, shredded (1 cup)
> 4 teaspoons grated Parmesan
>   cheese

A creamy, rich cheese sauce drenches these tasty Belgian Endive-Ham Rolls. To complete the meal, add a fruit salad and dessert.

Wash endive and trim bottoms. In small saucepan combine water, lemon juice, salt, and pepper. Add the endive. Cover; simmer for 10 minutes. Drain thoroughly.

Roll each endive stalk in 2 ham slices (put together to form a double thickness). Place rolls in bottom of a 10x6x1½-inch baking dish or 4 individual casseroles.

In saucepan melt butter over low heat; blend in flour. Stir in milk and chicken broth all at once. Cook and stir over low heat till mixture thickens and bubbles. Remove from heat; add American cheese and stir till cheese melts. Pour sauce over ham rolls.

Sprinkle with grated Parmesan cheese. Bake endive-ham rolls at 350° for 15 minutes or till heated through. Makes 4 servings.

Belgian endive is available from October to May. Select heads that are firm, white with a greenish tinge, and without blemish. This vegetable can be kept for a short time under refrigeration.

This tasty winter vegetable can be served cooked with any main dish. Raw endive can be used in a vegetable salad or stuffed for an appetizer. (See also *Endive.*)

BELL PEPPER—Another name for the sweet pepper. (See also *Pepper.*)

Bel Paese—
a mild cheese
from Italy.

BEL PAESE CHEESE *(bel′ pä ä′zä)*—A delicately flavored, soft, circular-shaped, Italian cheese with a slate gray surface and light yellow interior. The name means beautiful country and has been used to refer to Italy in classical and popular literature. It is no wonder that the name was transferred to this delicious cheese when it was developed around the turn of the century. Bel Paese cheese has made famous its town of origin, Melzo, Italy. Packages of cheese exported bear a map of Italy. Homemakers in the United States will find imported Bel Paese and domestic versions in a distinctive round, wooden container in supermarkets or specialty cheese shops. Wax-coated, foil-wrapped wedges of the cheese are also available.

This mild, buttery cheese is excellent served either as an appetizer or for dessert. It also melts readily and can be substituted for mozzarella in many Italian dishes. (See also *Cheese.*)

BELUGA CAVIAR—Largest-size grain or roe of the Russian caviars. This delicacy is obtained from the white or beluga sturgeon which is found in the Caspian and Black Seas. (See also *Caviar.*)

BENNE SEED—Another name by which Sesame seed is known. (See also *Sesame.*)

BERGAMOT—(1) A lemon-flavored herb of the mint family. It is a hardy perennial with dark green, fragrant leaves. The several varieties bear pretty, shaggy flowers ranging from white, pink, and pinkish lavender to deep red.

Bergamot is one of the few native American herbs and is commonly known by three other names, Monarda, bee balm, and Oswego tea. Each has an interesting background. Monarda comes from the plant's botanical name given because of its discoverer, Niccolo Monardes. He was a Spaniard who visited in the new world in the 16th century. The flowers of the bergamot plant are particularly fragrant and a great attraction to bees. It is not surprising, therefore, that the common name, bee balm, came into being.

The Oswego Indians used the dried leaves of the red bergamot for a beverage. American colonists who were boycotting English tea at the time of the Boston Tea Party showed their patriotism by serving Oswego or bergamot tea, instead.

Today the dried leaves and flowers can still be used to make an herb tea. Fresh sprigs of bergamot make a delightful garnish for an iced fruit beverage. Chopped leaves and flowers may be tossed with salad greens or sprinkled on cooked vegetables. (See also *Herb.*)

(2) A variety of winter pear known in the British Isles since Roman times.

(3) A variety of orange cultivated in southern Europe, especially Italy. It yields an essential oil used in the confectionery and perfume industries. The bergamot orange peel is sometimes candied and used in fancy pastries.

BERRY—A fleshy or pulpy fruit without a stone but with a few or many seeds imbedded in the pulp. Currants, blueberries, and cranberries are examples of true berries. In common usage, berry refers to many more fruits including strawberries, blackberries, and raspberries, which do not fit a precise botanical definition.

Wild berries were important in ancient man's diet long before he knew how to grow crops. This saga of living off nature was repeated as settlers crossed the Atlantic and struggled to survive in a new land. The pilgrims found blackberries, blueberries, barberries, raspberries, elderberries, mulberries, cranberries, and strawberries in the woods and wild areas adjacent to their new home. These berries were eaten fresh or stewed. They were made, also, into jams and jellies for future use. Drying was another means of preserving these delicious fruits for enjoyment during the long winter months.

As the frontier moved westward, hunters and trappers took advantage of wild berries to supplement the food supply they carried with them. Because these hardy men traveled light, dried meat and pemmican were the mainstays of their diet. The latter was usually made from buffalo meat which was dried and pounded fine, then mixed with fat and pulverized wild berries such as sheepberries. It was concentrated food flavored with berries.

The pioneers and their families following the trail blazers covered the land with gardens and farms. The women of this era made fresh pies and "put up" preserves from the berry patch in their garden plus whatever wild berries could be found. They also made berry wine, especially if elderberries were available nearby.

In the ensuing years horticultural advances have improved the quality and added to the number of varieties of berries marketed. Loganberries and boysenberries are two hybrids that have become especially popular. The long, reddish loganberries are a cross between blackberries and red raspberries. Boysenberries, large and dark with a raspberrylike flavor, were developed from three varieties of blackberries, a raspberry, and a loganberry. The olallie berry is a recent blackberry variety.

Berries are native to many climates. Many varieties are related and from time to time the names are interchanged. The blueberry is a good example. Blueberries are known throughout the world, but the large blueberries marketed in the United States are a horticultural development of the wild huckleberry. The seeds, rather than the color, are the clue to identification. Blueberries contain a number of tiny, fine seeds while each huckleberry contains ten fairly large, hard seeds.

Lingonberries, so popular with Scandinavian cooks, are a type of small cranberry that thrives in the climate of those northern countries. Wild dewberries are related to the blackberry although the plants on which they grow differ.

Nutritive value: Berries as a group contain varying amounts of vitamins A, C, and thiamine. Strawberries are the highest of the group in vitamin C content.

The bright color of berries as well as their tart to sweet flavor add a great deal of eating enjoyment at any meal. Served fresh without sugar, they are relatively low in calories per serving. However, since berries are often used in pies or preserves, all of which are heavily sweetened, calories increase accordingly.

How to select: With the exception of strawberries, all mature berries should be without a hull. In general, the type of berry being purchased should be plump, firm, and full-colored. Fresh berries with soft spots, mold, or other visible blemishes should be avoided.

Fresh strawberries are available all year but are in greatest supply during May and June. Other berries have a shorter market season. Blueberries come to market from May through September but are most plentiful in June, July, and August. The cranberry season is September through December. Most other types of berries are available only briefly in local markets during June and July.

Wild berries are scarce but occasionally can be found on camping trips or visits to the country. However, the shopper today is blessed with canned and frozen berries the year round to supplement those she buys fresh during the short growing seasons.

How to store: Almost all berries are perishable. Depending upon the degree of ripeness, these fruits will keep a few days lightly covered in the refrigerator. Berries are at peak quality when served immediately after purchase or picking.

Since dampness hastens deterioration of the fruit, berries should not have water clinging to them when they go into the refrigerator. Most homemakers wait to wash the berries until just before serving time. Others prefer to wash the berries and then spread them out on paper toweling to dry before storing.

Fortunately berries freeze well with either a sugar or syrup pack. Some berries, such as cranberries and blueberries, are very satisfactory when frozen unsweetened. Personal preference and future serving plans for the berries will determine which method is the most practical.

How to use: Versatile berries find favor in every phase of meal planning. As an appetizer they bring contrast in color and shape to other components of a fruit cup. Commercially bottled cranberry juice and other berry-juice drinks make a refreshing change as the first course of a meal. These same beverages are also welcome additions to a punch bowl.

At breakfast fresh berries are flavorful toppers for crisp cereal. Homemakers find that blueberry muffins or pancakes always rate an early morning smile. For those who prefer berries on top of rather than inside the pancake batter, there is a tempting array of berry syrups for just such eating enjoyment. Boysenberry joins strawberry, raspberry, and blueberry in this group. They are tasty on waffles and French toast too. And, who can resist strawberry or raspberry jam or currant jelly on hot buttered toast or English muffins?

The luncheon salad is another menu-pleasing use for berries, whether fresh ones are in season or not. Canned and frozen berries add their touch of the rainbow to fancy molded salads or tempting fruit plate combinations.

Although no turkey dinner is complete without cranberry sauce, enjoyment of this ruby-hued relish is not limited to poultry. Roast pork and smoked ham are two meats which benefit from a cranberry accompaniment. Currant jelly is melted with wine, orange peel, and spices to make the regal Cumberland Sauce which is served with ham and game.

Berries such as juniper are used as an herb or seasoning. Hunters know that crushed juniper berries cooked with wild game will overcome some of the gamey flavor and pleasantly season the roast. The juniper berry is valuable commercially, too, for it is an indispensible ingredient in the manufacture of gin.

The list of berry desserts is long and luscious. It begins with a bowl of berries and cream and continues through delicate Bavarian and angel desserts. In between are puddings and dumplings, ice creams and sherbets, pies, parfaits, sundae sauces, and shortcakes.

Fresh berries such as currants and elderberries are most often made into jams and jellies. Others, like fresh strawberries which are plentiful, and gooseberries, raspberries, and blackberries which are scarce, are made into preserves to be enjoyed long after the very short growing season. (See *Fruit*, and individual berry name for additional information.)

BETTY—A baked dessert made of sliced sweetened fruit and buttered bread crumbs. When brown sugar is used, the dessert is known as a brown betty. The fruit inside is tender and juicy and the top, brown and crisp. Often fruit juice or water is poured over the dessert before it goes into the oven. This assures the betty will be juicy when served.

Although many people use the names betty, fruit crisp, or crumble interchangeably, bread crumbs are the typical ingredients of a betty dessert. The others are topped with cereal or a crumbly mixture of butter, sugar, flour, and spices.

A betty may be prepared from many kinds of fruit. Apple betty is the most familiar. But this is probably because apples are plentiful and well liked. Berries, peaches, rhubarb, and plums are a few of the other possibilities. The fruit may be fresh, frozen, or canned. If syrup-packed fruit is used, less sugar will be needed.

Sunny lemon sauce and whipped cream top the spicy goodness of Apple Butter Betty served warm and fragrant from the oven.

Cream or ice cream accompanies a fruit betty. Lemon sauce is another popular topper. (See also *Dessert*.)

Honey Rhubarb Betty

> 1 pound rhubarb, cut in ½-inch slices (about 4 cups)
> ¾ cup sugar
> 2 tablespoons water
> 1 teaspoon ground nutmeg
>   Dash salt
> ½ cup honey
> 6 tablespoons butter or margarine, melted
> 5 slices bread, cut in cubes (about 4 cups)

Combine rhubarb, sugar, water, nutmeg, and salt in 10x6x1½-inch baking dish. Blend honey and butter; stir in bread cubes. Spoon over top of rhubarb. Bake at 375° about 30 minutes, or till golden brown. Makes 4 to 6 servings.

Apple Butter Betty

> 1½ cups apple butter
> ½ cup butter or margarine, melted
> 2 teaspoons lemon juice
> 1 teaspoon vanilla
> 9 cups (10 slices) ½-inch soft bread cubes
> ¼ cup chopped walnuts
>   Lemon Sauce
>   Whipped cream

Combine first four ingredients. Add bread cubes and nuts; toss to coat evenly. Spread mixture in 10x6x1½-inch baking dish. Bake at 350° for 20 to 25 minutes. Serve warm with Lemon Sauce and whipped cream. Serves 6. To prepare *Lemon Sauce:* In small saucepan combine ⅔ cup sugar, 2 tablespoons cornstarch, and dash salt. Blend in 1 cup water. Cook over medium heat, stirring constantly, till mixture is thick and bubbly. Cook 2 minutes longer or until mixture is clear. Remove from heat. Add 2 tablespoons butter or margarine, 1 teaspoon grated lemon peel, and 2 tablespoons lemon juice. Stir till butter or margarine melts. Makes 1¼ cups sauce.

BEURRE *(boer')*—The French word for butter. Its presence on a menu as part of a term indicates that the sauce or dish listed is prepared with butter.

BEURRE MANIE *(boer' man yā)*—A French cooking term for a blend of unmelted butter and flour used to thicken gravy or stew. Generally the proportions are of equal parts butter and flour. Thus, one tablespoon of beurre manie will thicken one cup of liquid to a thin sauce consistency. Some chefs prefer to reduce the amount of butter so that the resulting sauce or gravy will be not quite as rich.

The flour and butter are creamed or kneaded together, sometimes with the fingers. Then it is divided into small balls of a measured amount such as a teaspoonful or a tablespoonful. The balls are refrigerated in a covered container until needed.

Adding the beurre manie is the final step in preparing the sauce or thickening the stew. The balls are dropped into the hot liquid one at a time, stirring constantly after each addition until the mixture reaches the desired thickness.

Keeping the liquid below the boiling point is the secret to success in using beurre manie. Rapid boiling may cause the sauce to separate. It is important, however, that the mixture be heated thoroughly for several minutes. This heating not only gives the mixture an opportunity to thicken sufficiently, but also cooks the flour so that the raw starch taste is eliminated.

It will be noted that one of the ways beurre manie differs from a roux is that the flour and butter are not cooked together before use. In a roux they are.

BEURRE NOIR *(boer' nwär')*—A French term literally meaning black butter but designating a very dark browned butter sauce for fish. Melted butter is allowed to remain over heat until it is a rich brown color. Despite its name, the butter is not allowed to blacken or burn.

BEURRE NOISETTE *(boer' nwä zet')*—A French term for melted butter browned to the color of a nut and served sizzling hot. Buerre noisette is not as dark in color as beurre noir.

BEVERAGE

*When and how to serve the myriad of beverages,
and how they fit into today's diet.*

Beverage is the general term for all types of liquid used for drinking. It includes nonalcoholic and alcoholic drinks, and water, undoubtedly the most common beverage.

The list of beverages is long and includes the nonalcoholic ades, carbonated beverages, colas, sodas and mixes, chocolate and cocoa drinks, coolers, eggnogs, fresh and frozen fruit juices, nectars, vegetable juices, milk, malted milks, ice cream drinks, punches, sodas, coffees of various kinds, and tea. The alcoholic beverages include beers, wines, champagnes, and the compounded and distilled beverages.

The origins of some of the beverages can be traced far into history. While the beginnings of many beverages are known, those of wine are lost in pre-history, although this is probably man's oldest alcoholic beverage. For example, wine is mentioned many times in the *Holy Bible,* both in the Old Testament and in the New Testament. Beer is another one of the alcoholic beverages which dates back many centuries, in this case, to the ancient Babylonians.

But it is not only the alcoholic beverages which date back in history. Some of the nonalcoholic beverages do so, too. Coffee is presumed to have been discovered in Arabia, while tea was discovered around 2700 B.C. according to Chinese folklore. It is not possible to date all beverages though it is worth noting that an unsweetened, cold version of cocoa was the royal drink of the Incas and Aztecs.

Beverages to suit every taste

←Keep refreshed with Cranberry Cooler, Mint Limeade, Fruited Iced Tea, Raspberry Crush, or Spiced Pineapple Sparkle.

Of the many beverages available in the United States, beer, tea, coffee, and milk rank high on the list.

Beer is understood to have been one of the common drinks of the first settlers. Other beverages enjoyed by the early colonists were whey, cider (in those days, alcoholic), and applejack (alcoholic). But, probably the Indians made the earliest beverages—maple drinks.

The colonists first started using tea around 1670. This beverage was more popular than coffee until the English king levied a tax on the beverage, resulting in the Boston Tea Party. Since that time, coffee has been the more popular nonalcoholic beverage of the two in America.

Milk, usually thought of as a food rather than a drink, is perhaps the most important beverage next to water. The first settlers in America were quick to realize the nutritional value of milk. Pilgrims landing in Plymouth brought no cattle with them. As a result, the death rate, particularly of young children, was high. This was attributed to the shortage of milk and nutritious food. Later settlers brought cows with them from England.

Role in diet: The body contains about 55 to 65 percent water by weight. It is present in every body cell and tissue. With this in mind, it is clear that water is second in importance only to oxygen to maintain life in the human body. Water is continually being lost by the body through respiration, perspiration, and elimination. It is replaced by water found in food and beverages. The body's need for water is influenced by climate and physical activity.

When the water content of the body is decreased, the sensation of thirst will appear. The only way to alleviate this is to consume some type of liquid. Normally, the amount of water that is needed is maintained unconsciously. Exceptions to this occur in infants and those who are ill. Good examples of thirst quenchers include tart beverages, such as lemonade, and carbonated beverages which are not too sweet.

But beverages are not only necessary to relieve thirst, they also play many vital roles in the body functions. They give energy, aid digestion and assimilation, and help in the regulation of heat and in the elimination of body waste. In addition, plain drinking water often contains some minerals needed by the body—calcium, iron, iodine, and sodium.

Some weight reduction diets recommend an increase in the amount of liquid consumed with or before a meal. These diets are based on the premise that an increase in liquid intake lessens the appetite causing a reduction in food intake. Other weight control programs omit or decrease the amount of liquid included in the meal.

Beverages can also act as a mild stimulant. Tea, coffee, chocolate, and cocoa all contain caffeine, a stimulant. For this reason, it is not always recommended to give tea and coffee to children. On the other hand the caffeine level is so low in cocoa and chocolate that these beverages are usually not harmful to children.

Use in menu

There are about as many ways to use and serve beverages as there are beverages. With a little imagination, the beverage can be an outstanding part of the menu rather than just a dull, unexciting accompaniment that is served with the meal.

Choosing the right cup or glass for each beverage is important, too. For ease in handling, hot beverages are usually served in mugs or cups with handles and the cups usually require saucers. For a conversation starter, serve coffee in a collection of attractive, unmatched mugs.

Demitasse cups are the small cups used for black coffee usually served after dinner. Since the demitasse coffee is strong, only small servings are needed. Tea, in the Oriental style, is often served in small cups without handles or saucers.

Serve small amounts of brandy in snifters. The brandy is warmed by the hands which cradle the glass. For cold cocktails with no ice, use stemmed glasses to keep the heat of the hands from warming the drink. To help keep drinks cold, chill the glass in the refrigerator or fill with crushed ice while the drink is being mixed. Then, empty the glass and pour in the drink, filling glass two-thirds full. Serve thirst quenchers, such as fruit ades, iced tea, iced coffee, and highballs in tall glasses to allow extra room for the ice.

Frosty glasses make cool-looking drinks and it's a special touch that is not difficult. To achieve the effect, chill glasses in the refrigerator or bury them in shaved ice till the glass is white and frosty. Be sure to provide coasters or napkins to protect tabletops from dripping glasses.

For a sweet-frosted rim on glasses, moisten a chilled glass with lemon or lime juice, then dip the rim in sugar.

Beverage cups and glasses

This list includes some of the most commonly used cups and glasses for beverages of all types and their average sizes, given in ounces. Use it as a guide for the amount of beverage to buy or prepare.

Demitasse cup .... 2 to 2½ ounces
Tea cup .... 6 ounces
Punch cup .... 6 ounces
Coffee cup .... 8 ounces
Fruit juice glass .... 5 ounces
Tumbler .... 8 to 12 ounces
Milk glass .... 12 ounces
Soft drink glass .... 12 ounces
Water goblet .... 11 to 15 ounces
Pony .... 1 ounce
Jigger .... 1½ ounces
Cordial glass .... 1 ounce
Sherry glass .... 4 to 5 ounces
Wine glass .... 8 to 10 ounces
Cocktail glass .... 4 to 6 ounces
Champagne glass .... 6 to 10 ounces
Old-fashioned glass .... 7½ ounces
Highball glass .... 8 to 12 ounces
Beer glass .... 10 ounces and larger

As an appetizer: Beverages can be served before a breakfast, brunch, or dinner party. If a cocktail hour precedes dinner, it is best to mix only one type of cocktail, then offer bourbon or scotch. And, don't forget those who do not drink. Provide fruit or vegetable juices, such as cranberry juice cocktail or vegetable juice cocktail, or a carbonated beverage.

It's best to stick to one of these cocktails before the dinner—martinis, manhattans, daiquiris, whiskey sours, or old-fashioneds. Remember to follow the exact proportions called for in the drink recipe for a successful outcome each time. Keep in mind that the gin and rum cocktails are especially good during hot summer months.

Sometimes wine can be offered instead of a cocktail. Good choices are dry sherry, vermouth, champagne, or a champagne cocktail. Serve these beverages cold and in the appropriate glassware.

When it's time for dinner to begin, a good first course is an appetizer beverage. The beverage that is picked to start the meal is very important, because if it is too sweet, bland, or too hot, the taste senses will be dulled and the remainder of the meal will not be enjoyed. Choose an appetizer beverage that is sharp and well-flavored so that it will be a stimulator. Be sure to plan the appetizer in conjunction with the rest of the menu. In this manner, foods will not be similar or duplicated in the following courses. Variation in flavors, textures, and temperatures of foods will make the entire meal exciting.

Two-Tone Cocktail is sure to bring many comments. You'll drink tomato juice, then a juice blend, followed with pineapple juice.

Two-Tone Cocktail

    4 cups chilled pineapple juice
    4 cups chilled tomato juice
    4 thin lemon slices, halved

Into each 8-ounce glass, pour ½ cup pineapple juice. Then tip glass and *slowly* pour ½ cup tomato juice down side of glass. Float lemon slices atop. Trim with sprigs of watercress, if desired. Makes 8 servings.

Note: To fix drinks ahead of time, store in the refrigerator; use within 1 hour.

Herbed Cocktail

    1 12-ounce can vegetable
        juice cocktail (1½ cups)
    1 13¾-ounce can chicken
        broth (1¾ cups)
    1 or 2 drops bottled hot pepper
        sauce
    ¼ teaspoon dried basil leaves,
        crushed

In saucepan combine vegetable juice cocktail, chicken broth, hot pepper sauce, and basil. Bring to boiling; simmer 10 minutes. Serve hot. Top each serving with a pat of butter or margarine, if desired. Makes 6 servings.

❋MENU❋

DINNER FOR THE BOSS

Two-Tone Cocktail or *Herbed Cocktail*

Roast Beef Tenderloin

Duchess Potatoes

Asparagus Spears

Lettuce Wedge   Italian Dressing

Bananas Foster

Coffee   Tea

Don't let the appetizer beverage steal the show and compete with the main course. It should not be so highly seasoned that the taste of the main dish is overpowered, and it should not be too filling, especially if a hearty entrée will follow.

Planning a beverage appetizer is wise because beverages are easy to prepare and serve. A chilled drink can usually be made ahead of time and refrigerated till it is served. This eliminates much of the last minute preparation.

Choose from a variety of fruit juices and serve them alone or in combination with other fruit juices. Use fresh, frozen, or canned products. Some ideas for fruit juice appetizers are cranberry, apple, grape, and prune; or apricot, peach, or pear nectar. Fresh vegetable juice cocktails made in electric vegetable juicers are also good as meal beginners, especially when served icy cold over ice cubes.

Appetizer Juices

• Combine 2 parts chilled tomato juice and 1 part sauerkraut juice. Serve over ice.
• Combine one 7-ounce bottle lemon-lime carbonated beverage with 1 cup pineapple juice. Dash with bitters.
• Mix equal parts cranberry juice cocktail and orange juice. Chill thoroughly.
• Heat canned vegetable juice cocktail. Stir in 1 teaspoon butter for each cup juice.
• Combine pineapple juice and orange juice. Trim glass with a lime wedge.
• Garnish grapefruit juice with a mint sprig.
• To each cup pineapple-grapefruit juice, add 2 whole cloves and 1 inch stick cinnamon. Simmer 5 minutes. Serve warm.

For a change, serve appetizers in unusual containers such as champagne or parfait glasses, or brandy snifters. Then, garnish the drink for a final touch. Fruity stirrers make attractive garnishes. Thread melon balls, pineapple chunks, fresh strawberries, tangerine sections, maraschino cherries, or other fruit on long wooden picks or bamboo skewers and use as swizzle sticks in the beverages. Rose geranium leaves also make attractive trims.

As an accompaniment: Today, beverages are served when preference demands. Some people like the beverage with the meal while others prefer it with dessert or after dinner. As with appetizer beverages to avoid repeating flavors, drinks that accompany the meal should be planned along with the rest of the menu. They should not be so highly flavored and filling that the rest of the meal cannot be appreciated, nor should the beverages that are chosen be so sweet that the appetite is stifled.

The beverages most commonly served with the meal as accompaniments are coffee, tea, and milk. The most healthful beverage choice for everyone of all ages is milk. The suggested amount of milk for children is three to four cups per day, for teen-agers four or more cups a day, and for adults two or more cups per day.

Coffee, a practically calorie-free drink when taken black, is no doubt the beverage requested most often by adults with their meal. No matter when it is served—breakfast, brunch, lunch, or dinner—a good cup of coffee, generally, will hit the spot. Individual preference dictates whether coffee contains cream and/or sugar, so have them on hand for company meals.

Substitute Coffee Aloha for the dessert when the meal is especially filling. Coconut adds a special flavor to the coffee.

Tea is another beverage that makes a good meal accompaniment. When the weather is warm, iced beverages taste particularly good. Both iced coffee and iced tea are excellent meal partners. Ever since iced tea was first made in 1904 at the St. Louis Exposition, it has been a favorite summertime beverage.

Other special occasions, like a picnic in the park or at the beach, or a backyard barbecue, call for special beverages to go along with the meal. Lemonade and limeade are popular favorites, as are soft drinks and carbonated beverages. Avoid beverages that are too sweet. They have a tendency to dull the appetite.

❈MENU❈

SUMMERTIME LUNCHEON

Creamed Chicken in Patty Shells
Molded Vegetable Salad
Ice Cream Sundae   Sugar Cookies
Fruited Iced Tea

❈MENU❈

COOKOUT FEAST

Grilled Cheeseburgers on Buns
Kidney Bean Salad
Potato Chips
Banana Cake
Mint Limeade   or   Raspberry Cooler

Fruited Iced Tea

2 tablespoons instant tea powder
5 cups cold water
1 cup light corn syrup
½ cup orange juice
½ cup lime juice
Lime slices
Maraschino cherries

Combine tea powder and water; stir till tea is dissolved. Add corn syrup, orange juice, and lime juice. Mix thoroughly. Chill. Serve over ice in tall glasses. Garnish with lime slices and maraschino cherries. Makes 8 servings.

Many people prefer wine as an accompaniment to a meal. While there are countless rules governing your choice of wine, the basic rules are to serve a dry wine with the main courses. Save the sweet red or white wine for dessert since it takes the edge off the appetite if served before or during the meal. The following are guides and personal taste should be the deciding factor as to which wine is served. Dry red wines are best with meats, game, and highly seasoned food. Dry white wines are best with poultry, fish, and seafood.

Mint Limeade

1 6-ounce can frozen limeade
   concentrate
½ cup lightly packed fresh mint
   leaves
2 tablespoons confectioners'
   sugar

Reconstitute limeade concentrate according to can directions. Combine mint leaves and confectioners' sugar; crush with a fork. Add to limeade; cover and let stand 30 minutes; strain. Tint to desired color with green food coloring. Serve over ice cubes or cracked ice. Garnish each serving with additional fresh mint leaves, if desired. Makes 4 servings.

Raspberry Cooler

Take plenty along on the picnic—

Dissolve one ½-ounce envelope unsweetened raspberry-flavored soft drink powder and ¾ cup sugar in 4 cups water. Add ½ cup orange juice, ¼ cup lemon juice, and one 12-ounce can (1½ cups) pineapple juice. Chill thoroughly. Serve over ice cubes. Makes 1½ quarts.

As a dessert: Sometimes a beverage that is on the sweet side can be served as the dessert, either hot or cold. Many of the ice cream beverages, such as sodas, malts, shakes, and floats can double as refreshers and desserts. Some chocolate beverages make good dessert drinks and in addition, are not too filling. A flavored tea or coffee would also be a delightful end to a full-sized meal for those individuals who are watching their caloric intake.

```
╭──────────────────────────────╮
│          ❈MENU❈              │
│                              │
│      OVEN-GOING  DINNER       │
│          Meat Loaf            │
│       Scalloped Potatoes      │
│   Assorted Vegetable Relishes │
│       Molded Fruit Salad      │
│  Tropical Chocolate  or  Coffee Aloha │
│      or Instant Russian Tea   │
╰──────────────────────────────╯
```

Tropical Chocolate

  1 quart milk
  6 tablespoons pre-sweetened instant
      cocoa powder
  1 ripe banana, cut in pieces
  ½ teaspoon vanilla

In blender container combine 1 *cup* milk, cocoa, and banana. Cover; blend till smooth. (Or, mash banana. Blend with 1 *cup* milk and cocoa; beat with rotary beater.) Pour into saucepan; add vanilla and remaining milk. Heat. If desired, float marshmallow atop. Serves 4.

Coffee Aloha

Heat together one 3½-ounce can flaked coconut (1⅓ cups), 2 cups milk, and 2 tablespoons sugar in saucepan. Pour into blender container and liquefy; strain. Add 2 cups extra-strong coffee; reheat. Serve in cups topped with a dollop of whipped cream. Sprinkle with toasted coconut. Makes 6 servings.

Instant Russian Tea

  ½ cup orange-flavored instant
      breakfast drink powder
  ⅓ cup instant tea powder
  ¼ cup sugar
  3 tablespoons pre-sweetened
      lemonade mix (½ of 3-ounce
      envelope)
  ¼ teaspoon ground cinnamon
  ⅛ teaspoon ground cloves

Combine the breakfast drink powder, tea powder, sugar, lemonade mix, cinnamon, and cloves. Add 8 cups boiling water; stir. Pour into teapot. Serve immediately. Serves 10.

As a refreshment: Many types of beverages are also consumed between meals, whether it be during the refrigerator raid for carbonated beverages or beer, or at a formal reception where all three—coffee, tea, and punch—can be served.

The type of beverage and food that is served depends on the occasion, personal taste, and size of the guest list. For example, an afternoon get-together to welcome a new neighbor might consist of an ice cream soda or lemonade and sugar cookies, while the larger formal tea could include dainty sandwiches, fancy cookies, candies, and nuts with coffee and punch.

But whatever type of party, it is important to keep the food simple and easy to handle with a balance of sweet and not so sweet foods. This is particularly true for the larger gatherings where more types of foods and beverages are served.

In addition to planning for company, have ingredients on hand in the freezer and refrigerator for the family to make their own between-meal snacks. Milk and ice cream drinks and fruit and vegetable juices, such as lemonade, not only taste good but are nutritious, too.

Punch that's simple to prepare

Toast the New Year with Cranberry Spar-→ kle, a refreshing and easy punch. Trim with maraschino cherries and citrus fruit slices.

AFTERNOON SNACK
Cherry Sparkle
or
Apple Frost
Butter Cookies

Cherry Sparkle

Combine one envelope unsweetened cherry-flavored soft drink powder and 1 cup sugar. Dissolve in 2 cups milk. Pour into 6 to 8 soda glasses. Using 1 quart vanilla ice cream and one 28-ounce bottle chilled carbonated water, add scoops of ice cream to glasses. Carefully pour in the carbonated water. Stir to muddle slightly. Makes 6 to 8 servings.

Apple Frost

Beat 1 pint lime sherbet till softened and smooth. Gradually stir in 1½ cups chilled apple juice, blending well. Serve immediately. Makes six ½-cup servings.

Weather also affects the beverage that is served. A chilly afternoon or evening calls for a warm drink—hot chocolate, hot spiced wine, hot buttered rum, or hot tea beverages. (See *Coffee, Tea, Wines and Spirits* for additional information.)

SNOW SHOVELING BREAK
Spicy Orange Tea
or
Apple-Honey Tea
Assorted Doughnuts

Spicy Orange Tea

    10 whole cloves
     1 stick cinnamon, broken
    ⅓ cup honey
     1 cup orange juice
     4 tea bags
       Aromatic bitters

Combine 1 cup water, cloves, and cinnamon. Simmer covered for 10 minutes. Add honey, 1 cup water, and orange juice; bring to boiling. Remove from heat; add tea bags. Let steep, covered, for 5 minutes. Remove tea and spices. Dash in bitters to taste. Serve in cups with quartered orange slices. Serves 4 or 5.

Apple-Honey Tea

     1 12-ounce can frozen apple cider
       concentrate
     2 tablespoons instant tea powder
     1 tablespoon honey
    ½ teaspoon ground cinnamon

In medium saucepan reconstitute apple cider concentrate according to directions on can. Add instant tea powder, honey, and cinnamon. Stir to blend; heat through. Makes 1½ quarts.

Eggnog Royale

    ⅓ cup sugar
     2 egg yolks
     4 cups milk
     1 tablespoon instant coffee
       powder
     2 egg whites
     3 tablespoons sugar
     1 teaspoon vanilla
     1 pint chocolate ice cream

Beat ⅓ cup sugar into egg yolks; add milk, coffee powder, and ¼ teaspoon salt. Cook and stir over medium heat till mixture coats a metal spoon; cool. Beat egg whites till soft mounds form; gradually add 3 tablespoons sugar, beating till soft peaks form.

Fold egg whites and vanilla into custard mixture. Chill about 3 hours. Pour into punch bowl or individual cups; top with small scoops of chocolate ice cream. Makes 12 servings.

❧ MENU ❦

FIRESIDE GET-TOGETHER

Eggnog Royale
Fruitcake
Salted Mixed Nuts

Spiced Pineapple Sparkle

2/3 cup sugar
1½ cups water
6 inches stick cinnamon
12 whole cloves
1 46-ounce can pineapple
   juice (6 cups)
1½ cups orange juice
½ cup lemon juice
1 28-ounce bottle ginger
   ale, chilled (3½ cups)
Cinnamon sticks

In saucepan combine sugar, water, cinnamon, and cloves. Cover and simmer 15 minutes. Strain to remove spices. Set aside to cool.

Add pineapple juice, orange juice, and lemon juice; chill. Just before serving, pour over ice cubes in punch bowl. Resting bottle on rim of bowl, carefully pour in ginger ale. Ladle into glasses. Use cinnamon stick as a stirrer for each glass. Makes about 12 servings.

Cranberry Sparkle

A delightful beverage for the holidays—

1 16-ounce can jellied cranberry
   sauce
¾ cup orange juice
¼ cup lemon juice
1 28-ounce bottle ginger
   ale, chilled (3½ cups)

Beat cranberry sauce till smooth; stir in orange and lemon juices. Pour cranberry mixture over ice cubes in 2-quart pitcher or punch bowl. Resting bottle on rim, carefully pour in ginger ale. Makes 12 to 15 servings.

Cranberry Cooler

4 quarts cranberry-apple drink,
   chilled
½ cup honey
2 to 3 tablespoons rum flavoring
Ice Ring

Combine first 3 ingredients; stir till blended. Serve in punch bowl over a large piece of ice or an Ice Ring. Makes 30 servings.

For *Ice Ring:* Fill a 5½-cup ring mold to within ½ inch of top with water. Freeze. To unmold press a hot kitchen towel against mold. Unmold ring onto a baking sheet, then carefully slip it into the punch bowl.

Raspberry Crush

1 envelope unsweetened raspberry-
   flavored soft drink powder
1 cup sugar
4 cups cold water
1 6-ounce can frozen lemonade
   concentrate, thawed
1 10-ounce package frozen raspberries, thawed
1 28-ounce bottle lemon-lime
   carbonated beverage (3½ cups)

Combine soft drink powder and sugar. Add water; stir till soft drink powder and sugar are dissolved. Stir in thawed lemonade concentrate and raspberries. Chill.

Just before serving pour into punch bowl or pitcher. Resting bottle on rim, carefully pour in carbonated beverage. Serve over ice cubes in glasses. Makes 10 to 12 servings.

❧ MENU ❦

HOLIDAY OPEN HOUSE

Open-Face Sandwiches
Apples   Assorted Cheese
Christmas Cookies
Festive Candies
Punch

Small heads of Bibb lettuce are attractive served either whole or halved lengthwise to show the creamy white leaves in the center.

BIBB LETTUCE—A variety of lettuce in which the leaves are cup-shaped in appearance and have a soft, buttery feel. Named for Major John Bibb who developed it, Bibb lettuce has a sweet, delicate flavor. The deep rich green leaves blend into a creamy white near the core and are exceedingly tender, yet they have a distinct crispness. Today, much of the Bibb lettuce is grown commercially in greenhouses, making it a year-round vegetable.

It is best stored in a plastic bag in the refrigerator. For top eating quality, use it as soon as possible after buying.

The heads are small enough to serve whole as individual servings, accompanied only with a simple salad dressing. Or, you can combine the leaves with other greens for a tossed salad. (See also *Lettuce*.)

BICARBONATE OF SODA—Another name for baking soda. (See also *Baking Soda*.)

BIFTECK *(bif' tek)*—A French term meaning beefsteak. (See also *French Cookery*.)

BIND—A cooking term which describes the use of various ingredients used to thicken or hold together a food mixture before and after cooking. Raw eggs and bread crumbs are often used to bind a meat loaf or meat-ball mixture. Similarly, a thick white sauce is used to bind ingredients in preparing a meat or fish croquette mixture.

BINDENFLEISCH—A Swiss air-dried beef. Top-quality beef is pickled, then dried at high altitudes during the winter. When ripe, it is pressed into shape. Thinly sliced, it is served as an hors d'oeuvre.

BING CHERRY—A variety of dark, sweet cherries. Named Bing after a Chinese gardener, they are grown in Western states.

Fresh Bings are available on the market from May through August. When mature and at their peak of flavor, they range from deep maroon or mahogany red to black. They should be plump with a bright and glossy surface; stems should appear fresh.

Overripe cherries appear shriveled and dull with dried stems. Due to their dark color, decayed areas are sometimes difficult to detect. For home use, Bings should be refrigerated unwashed in plastic bags. Wash cherries just before serving.

Bings are delicious for out-of-hand eating or combined with other fruits for colorful salads or desserts. They are also excellent either canned or frozen for year-round enjoyment. (See also *Cherry*.)

Snowcap Cherry Nibbles

Combine 1 cup dairy sour cream, 2 tablespoons brown sugar, and ½ teaspoon shredded lemon peel. Refrigerate to blend flavors.

Surround bowls of sour cream dip, coarsely chopped pecans, and toasted coconut* with dark sweet cherries. Dip fruit in sour cream mixture, then in nuts or coconut. If desired, pass cocktail picks to spear fruit.

*Toasted coconut: Spread thin layer of coconut in shallow baking pan. Toast at 350° till lightly browned, 6 to 7 minutes. (Stir coconut or shake pan often to toast evenly.)

Summer refreshment

For delectable Snowcap Cherry Nibbles, dip →
plump, Bing cherries in sour cream, then in chopped pecans or toasted coconut.

Luncheon Salad

1 20½-ounce can pineapple chunks
2 12-ounce cartons cream-style
　　cottage cheese (3 cups)
1 cup halved pitted dark sweet
　　cherries
3 oranges, peeled and sectioned
1 banana, peeled and cut in
　　sixths*
1 cup halved seedless green
　　grapes
½ cup mayonnaise or salad
　　dressing
½ cup whipping cream, whipped

Drain pineapple, reserving ½ cup syrup. Arrange pineapple, cottage cheese, cherries, oranges, banana, and grapes on lettuce-lined plates. Prepare dressing by folding ½ cup reserved syrup and mayonnaise into whipped cream. Chill salads and dressing separately. At serving time, pass dressing. Makes 6 servings.

*To keep banana pieces attractive and bright, dip in ascorbic acid color keeper or dip in lemon juice mixed with a little water.

Creamy Fruit Combo

1 cup seedless green grapes
1 8¾-ounce can pineapple
　　tidbits, drained (⅔ cup)
1 cup pitted dark sweet cherries
1 cup diced orange
1 cup cantaloupe balls
2 medium plums, sliced
⅔ cup flaked coconut
　　　• • •
　　Creamy Dressing
1 cup sliced banana

Combine first 7 ingredients. Fold in Creamy Dressing. Chill 24 hours to allow flavors to blend fully. Fold in sliced banana just before serving. Makes 8 to 10 servings.

Creamy Dressing: In small saucepan combine 2 beaten eggs, 2 tablespoons orange juice, and 2 tablespoons vinegar; stir in ¼ cup sugar and dash salt. Cook over low heat, stirring constantly, till mixture thickens. Remove mixture from heat and stir in 1 tablespoon butter or margarine. Cool. Fold in 1 cup dairy sour cream. Chill dressing thoroughly.

BIRD PEPPER—A perennial, shrubby plant bearing a small, red vegetable. Extremely hot, bird peppers are used alone as a seasoning in some countries. In the United States, they are often used in combination with other ingredients in the making of bottled hot pepper sauce. (See also *Pepper*.)

BIRD'S NEST—The dried gelatinous substance produced by a type of swallow to aid her in building her nest. Available in specialty stores, bird's nest is used in preparing Bird's Nest Soup, considered a Chinese delicacy. It may also be used as a stuffing. (See also *Oriental Cookery*.)

BISCUIT—A small, light bread generally leavened with baking powder or baking soda. Classified as a quick bread, the soft dough is made of flour, liquid, fat, and leavening. It is shaped and cut into rounds or dropped in small pieces onto a baking sheet before baking. Other ingredients such as shredded cheese, grated fruit peel, or minced onion are often added.

Very thin wafers and other breadlike foods are called biscuits in some countries. The Europeans and English refer to crackers as biscuits. In addition, the English label cookies as sweet biscuits.

Types of biscuits: Regional preferences account for the different types of biscuits served in various parts of the United States. In the North, a tender biscuit with a flaky crumb and a large volume is preferred. Such a biscuit is achieved by using all-purpose flour which is high in gluten. Gluten is responsible for the elasticity of the dough and is developed by kneading.

A crusty biscuit with a soft, tender crumb which doesn't flake is popular in the South. A soft wheat flour is used to produce this type of biscuit. Baking soda is most often used as the leavening agent with buttermilk or sour milk added. The dough is handled as little as possible to avoid the development of gluten. It is generally rolled less than ½ inch thick.

Certain characteristics are considered standard for both types of biscuits. A good biscuit is symmetrical in shape with a fairly smooth, even top. The crust is tender, slightly crisp, free from excess flour, and golden brown. Although the texture varies depending upon the type, a good biscuit is creamy white inside with a slightly moist, tender crumb and pleasing flavor. In addition, the standard biscuit is lightweight in comparison to its size.

Beaten biscuits, popular in the South before the Civil War, have a very dry, brittle crumb. Unlike the more familiar biscuit, beaten biscuits do not contain a leavening agent. Instead, they are leavened by repeatedly pounding or beating the dough which in turn softens the gluten.

Preparing biscuits: The biscuit method for mixing ingredients is used not only for biscuits but also in making many other quick breads. Sift dry ingredients together into a bowl. Cut in shortening with a pastry blender, two knives, blending fork, or fingers until the mixture resembles coarse crumbs. (Work quickly if fingers are used to cut in shortening, as the warmth of the hands tends to soften the fat, making a sticky mixture difficult to handle.)

Form a well in the dry mixture, then add liquid all at once. Using a fork, stir quickly just till dough follows fork around the bowl forming a soft dough.

Turn out onto a lightly floured surface and knead gently 10 to 12 strokes. Roll or pat dough to a ½-inch thickness. Using a biscuit cutter, push cutter straight down without twisting. Uneven pressure will cause biscuits to be asymmetrical. Dip cutter in flour between each cut to prevent dough from sticking. Scraps of dough can be either patted or rerolled together and

Piping hot from the oven, Biscuits Supreme brighten any breakfast. Watch biscuits disappear down to the last crumb when spread generously with butter and drizzled with honey.

cut for additional biscuits. Unbaked biscuits may be refrigerated up to one hour before baking without loss of quality.

Biscuits are traditionally cut into rounds with straight-edge or crimped-edge cutters of various sizes. Tiny 1- to 1½-inch cutters may be used for tea biscuits. The 2- to 2½-inch size is best when biscuits are served at breakfast, lunch, or dinner.

An alternate method for cutting biscuits is to roll the dough into a square or rectangle. Using a sharp knife dipped in flour, cut the dough into squares, rectangles, or triangles. Be careful to avoid flattening dough when cutting or biscuits will be uneven after baking.

For crusty edges, place biscuits ¾ inch apart on ungreased baking sheet. For soft sides, place biscuits close together in a shallow baking pan. If desired, brush biscuit tops with milk or light cream before baking for a more golden color.

Drop biscuits are prepared according to the biscuit method except that a higher proportion of liquid to dry ingredients is used. The resulting mixture is a very thick batter rather than a soft dough. The biscuits are dropped by teaspoonfuls onto a greased baking sheet. As to be expected, drop biscuits vary somewhat in size. However, this method is faster for preparing biscuits when time is short.

Biscuit products: Commercially prepared biscuit mix is available on the market in various-sized packages. It contains flour, shortening, leavening, milk powder, salt, and sugar. For plain biscuits, water is added to the mix. For a richer, sweeter dough, additional sugar, shortening, and eggs may be added. The mix should be stored in a cool, dry place. It is convenient for making coffee cakes, short cakes, griddle cakes, and other quick breads.

Prepackaged refrigerated biscuits, also available on the market, eliminate all mixing. The biscuits only require baking before serving. The unbaked biscuits need refrigeration and should be used before the expiration date printed on the package. Various sized packages as well as different types of biscuits are available in this form. (See *Beaten Biscuit, Bread,* and *Drop Biscuit* for additional information.)

Biscuits Supreme

> 2 cups sifted all-purpose flour
> 4 teaspoons baking powder
> 2 teaspoons sugar
> ½ teaspoon salt
> ½ teaspoon cream of tartar
> ½ cup shortening
> ⅔ cup milk

Sift together first 5 ingredients. Cut in shortening till mixture resembles coarse crumbs. Make a well; add milk all at once. Stir just till dough clings together. Turn onto lightly floured surface. Knead gently 10 to 12 strokes. Roll or pat ½ inch thick. Cut with biscuit cutter; dip cutter in flour between cuts. Place on ungreased baking sheet. Bake at 450° for 10 to 12 minutes or till golden brown. Makes 16.

Whole Wheat Biscuits

> 1 cup sifted all-purpose flour
> 4 teaspoons baking powder
> ¾ teaspoon salt
> 1 cup whole wheat flour
> ¼ cup shortening
> ¾ cup milk

Sift together first 3 ingredients; stir in whole wheat flour. Cut in shortening till mixture resembles coarse crumbs. Make a well; add milk all at once. Stir just till dough clings together. Turn onto lightly floured surface. Knead gently 10 to 12 strokes. Roll or pat dough ½ inch thick. Dip cutter in flour; cut dough straight down without twisting. Place on ungreased baking sheet. Bake at 450° for 12 to 15 minutes or till lightly browned. Makes 16.

Cheese Breakfast Biscuits

Beat together one 3-ounce package cream cheese, softened; ¼ cup apricot preserves; 1 egg; and ½ teaspoon vanilla. Using 1 package refrigerated biscuits (10 biscuits), flatten each biscuit on ungreased baking sheet to a 3½-inch circle. Build up rim on sides of each biscuit. Spoon about 1 tablespoon cheese filling in center of each. Sprinkle ¼ cup chopped pecans over filled biscuits. Bake at 375° for 14 to 16 minutes. Serve warm. Makes 10.

Baking Powder Biscuits

 2 cups sifted all-purpose flour
 3 teaspoons baking powder
 ½ teaspoon salt
 ¼ cup shortening
 ¾ cup milk

Sift together flour, baking powder, and salt into bowl. Cut in shortening till mixture resembles coarse crumbs. Make a well; add milk all at once. Stir quickly with fork just till dough follows fork around bowl.

 Turn dough onto lightly floured surface. Knead gently 10 to 12 strokes. Roll or pat dough ½ inch thick. Dip biscuit cutter in flour; cut dough straight down without twisting. Place biscuits on ungreased baking sheet. Bake at 450° for 12 to 15 minutes. Makes 16.

Buttermilk Biscuits

 2 cups sifted all-purpose flour
 3 teaspoons baking powder
 ½ teaspoon salt
 ¼ teaspoon baking soda
 ⅓ cup shortening
 ¾ cup buttermilk

Sift together first 4 ingredients. Cut in shortening till mixture resembles coarse crumbs. Make a well; add buttermilk all at once. Stir just till dough clings together. Turn onto lightly floured surface. Knead gently 10 to 12 strokes. Roll or pat ½ inch thick. Dip cutter in flour; cut dough straight down without twisting. Place on ungreased baking sheet. Bake at 450° for 12 to 15 minutes. Makes 16.

Pecan Tea Biscuits

Sift together 1¾ cups sifted all-purpose flour, 3 tablespoons sugar, 2 teaspoons baking powder, and ½ teaspoon salt. Cut in ¼ cup shortening till mixture resembles coarse crumbs. Blend 1 beaten egg with ¾ cup milk. Add all at once to dry mixture, stirring just to moisten. Stir in ½ cup chopped pecans.

 Drop by heaping teaspoonfuls on greased baking sheet. Combine 2 tablespoons sugar and ½ teaspoon cinnamon; sprinkle over biscuits. Bake at 425° about 10 minutes. Makes 36.

Add liquid all at once to dry ingredients. Stir quickly with a fork just till mixture clings together, forming a soft dough.

On lightly floured surface, knead biscuit dough lightly, about 10 to 12 strokes. Pat or roll dough to a ½-inch thickness.

To cut biscuits, dip biscuit cutter in flour. Press straight down; avoid twisting cutter or flattening cut edges of biscuits.

BISCUIT TORTONI—A rich cream dessert frozen in small-cup portions, named after a former eating place in Paris—the Café Tortoni. This frozen dessert generally contains crumbled macaroons, whipped cream, confectioners' sugar, chopped almonds, and maraschino cherries. It is sometimes additionally flavored with rum or sherry. (See also *Dessert*.)

Biscuit Tortoni

A delicate almond flavor makes this dessert extra special—

> 1 cup crumbled soft macaroons
>   (5 cookies)
> ¼ cup confectioners' sugar
> ¾ cup light cream
>   •   •   •
> 1 teaspoon vanilla
> Few drops almond extract
> 1 cup whipping cream
>   •   •   •
> Maraschino cherries, halved
> Toasted chopped almonds

In bowl combine crumbled macaroons, confectioners' sugar, and light cream. Let stand for 1 hour. Stir in vanilla and almond extract.

Whip cream until soft peaks form. Fold in macaroon mixture. Pour into individual paper bake cups placed in muffin pans. Garnish tops with maraschino cherries and chopped almonds. Freeze till firm. Makes 10 servings.

BISMARCK—A raised doughnut, either round or pillow-shaped, that has been filled with jelly. A traditional German food, these jelly doughnuts were named after a German statesman who was particularly popular with Berliners.

The doughnut may be filled with jelly before or after baking. If filled before baking, the dough is rolled thinly and cut into small rounds or rectangles. A small amount of jelly or jam is placed in the center of half of the circles; then the remaining circles are placed over the jelly to encase the filling. The edges are pinched together tightly to prevent jelly from seeping out. The doughnuts are deep-fat fried until golden brown. After frying they may be coated with granulated or confectioners' sugar, if desired, before serving.

Another method for preparing Bismarcks is to slit the cooked doughnut and fill with jelly. With this method, the dough is rolled slightly thicker than in the method mentioned above, and the jelly or jam is inserted through a very small puncture made in the side of the doughnut after deep-fat frying. (See also *Doughnut*.)

Quick Bismarcks

A shortcut method for a jelly-filled treat—

> 1 package refrigerated biscuits
>   (10 biscuits)
> Jelly *or* jam
> Fat for frying
> Confectioners' sugar

Flatten each biscuit to ¼-inch thickness. Place about 1 teaspoon jelly or jam on *half* of the flattened biscuits. Cover with remaining biscuits; pinch edges together, sealing well.

Fry filled biscuits in deep hot fat (375°) about 3 minutes on each side or till golden brown. Drain on paper toweling. Dust with confectioners' sugar. Serve warm. Makes 5.

BISQUE *(bisk)*—A rich, thick, velvety smooth soup generally made with cream and a shellfish base. Authoritative sources indicate that seafood has not always been the only meat used in a bisque. During the eighteenth and nineteenth centuries recipes for using other kinds of meat, poultry, and game such as quail or pigeon in bisque were popular. Bread crumbs along with the meat puree were added to thicken the soup. The final step in many of these rich, meaty soups was the addition of a crayfish purée to the bisque before serving.

A true bisque made with crab, clam, shrimp, or lobster requires many hours to prepare. The shellfish is first marinated overnight in a court bouillon of water, dry white wine, and seasonings. The seafood is then cooked in the bouillon with fresh tomatoes until tender. Next the mixture is strained and the solids are sieved to make a very smooth purée. Then the purée is returned to the bouillon. Cream, breadcrumbs, and sherry or brandy are sometimes added. The bisque is seasoned and simmered until ready to serve.

Today, the term bisque has expanded to include cream soups made with a purée of vegetables and/or seafood. Futhermore, bits of food are often found in the soup. Thus, a broader meaning has developed with shortcut cookery. (See also *Soup*.)

Seafood Bisque

  1 10½-ounce can condensed clam
      chowder (New England-style)
  1 14½-ounce can evaporated milk
      (1⅔ cups)
  1 3-ounce can chopped mushrooms,
      undrained (⅔ cups)
  1 7½-ounce can crab meat,
      drained, flaked, and cartilage
      removed
  ¼ cup dry sherry
      Butter or margarine

In saucepan combine chowder with milk; heat just to boiling. Stir in undrained mushrooms and crab. Heat through. Stir in sherry just before serving. To serve, float butter pat atop each serving and garnish with parsley, if desired. Makes 4 or 5 servings.

Crab Bisque

  1 10½-ounce can condensed
      cream of mushroom soup
  1 10½-ounce can condensed
      cream of asparagus soup
  1½ soup cans milk (2 cups)
  1 cup light cream
  1 7½-ounce can crab meat,
      drained, flaked, and cartilage
      removed
  ¼ cup dry white wine
      Butter or margarine

Blend together mushroom and asparagus soups; stir in milk and cream. Heat just to boiling. Add crab; heat through. Stir in wine just before serving. Float butter pat atop soup and garnish with parsley, if desired. Serves 6 to 8.

BITOK *(bē tôk')*—A small, Russian meat patty or cake prepared from a ground meat mixture similar to that used by Americans in making a meat loaf. Almost any kind of meat (beef, veal, pork, mutton, chicken, or rabbit) can be ground for the preparation of bitok. Milk-soaked bread and finely chopped onion are added to the ground meat. The grinding process is repeated until a very smooth mixture results. It is then shaped into little round cakes about 1½ inches in diameter. The cakes are floured and browned in butter, then simmered in sour cream for a few minutes before serving. (See also *Russian Cookery*.)

BITTER ORANGE—The fruit produced by a tree of the same name. Although some sources indicate the tree is a native of India, it is more probable that it originated in South China and the Indo-Chinese peninsula. The bitter orange was brought from Palestine into Italy by the Crusaders. It was introduced into Spain, southern France, and East Africa by the Arabs.

Oil from the flowers and leaves of the bitter orange tree is used in preparing some aromatic flavorings. And, the dried peel from the bitter Seville orange is used in making orange-flavored bitters often added to mixed drinks. (See also *Orange*.)

Creamy Crab Bisque is a snap to make. An adaptation of the traditional seafood soup, it uses canned soup to eliminate many steps.

BITTERS—Aromatic liquids with a bitter taste made from various combinations of roots, barks, herbs, and leaves. Essences of cloves, quinine, juniper, myrrh, cardamom, cinnamon, mace, and the dried peel of bitter oranges are only a few of the substances used in the secret recipes. In addition, many bitters contain alcohol.

Bitters were originally used medicinally and some still claim to aid digestion. Others serve as an appetite stimulant while many are used to flavor foods or mixed drinks. In Europe, bitters are often labeled as aperitifs. When used as a flavoring, generally only a dash or two of bitters is needed. (See also *Wines and Spirits*.)

Apricot Swizzle

> 4 teaspoons instant tea powder
> 1/4 cup sugar
> 1 12-ounce can apricot nectar
>   (1 1/2 cups)
> 1/2 teaspoon aromatic bitters
> 1 6-ounce can frozen lemonade
>   concentrate, thawed
> 1 28-ounce bottle ginger ale,
>   chilled (3 1/2 cups)

Mix tea, sugar, nectar, bitters, and 2 cups cold water; stir till sugar dissolves. Just before serving add concentrate and several ice cubes; stir. Slowly add ginger ale; mix gently. Serves 8.

Tropic Isle Appetizer

> 1 1/2 cups pineapple juice, chilled
> 1/2 cup orange juice, chilled
> 2 drops aromatic bitters
> 1 7-ounce bottle ginger ale,
>   chilled (about 1 cup)
> 1/2 pint pineapple sherbet

Combine chilled pineapple juice and orange juice; stir in aromatic bitters. Divide among 4 chilled glasses. Tip each glass and slowly pour ginger ale down side to fill. Top each serving with a scoop of pineapple sherbet. If desired, thread fresh fruit (strawberries, pineapple chunks, melon balls) on glass straws for kabob stirrers. Garnish each appetizer with a sprig of fresh mint, if desired. Makes 4 servings.

BLACK BEAN—A variety of dried beans often called turtle beans. Oval in shape and smaller than the popular red kidney bean, the black bean has a whitish inside with a distinctive flavor of its own.

Widely used in South America, black beans are included in many Brazilian dishes. Here in the United States, Black Bean Soup is a popular Southern dish.

In addition to soups, black beans are used in dips and main dishes. As with other dried vegetables, they should be soaked overnight before cooking. They are available in some specialty stores and regional markets in dried form as well as canned and in soups. If not available, red beans may be used in recipes. (See also *Bean*.)

Black Bean Soup

> 1 pound dried black beans
>   (2 1/2 cups)
> Ham bone with meat
> 2 medium onions, chopped (1 cup)
> 2 stalks celery, chopped (1 cup)
> 2 carrots, chopped (1/2 cup)
> 1/4 cup snipped parsley
> 1 tablespoon Worcestershire sauce
> 1/2 teaspoon dry mustard
> 2 whole bay leaves
> 3 whole cloves
> Dash dried thyme leaves,
>   crushed
> • • •
> 1/4 cup dry sherry
> 2 hard-cooked eggs, sliced
> Thin lemon slices

Rinse beans. Soak overnight in 6 cups cold water; *or*, bring beans and water to boiling. Simmer for 2 minutes; let stand at least 1 hour.

Drain beans, discarding liquid. Add next 10 ingredients and 7 cups water. Bring to boiling; reduce heat. Simmer, covered, for 2 to 2 1/2 hours or till beans are very tender.

Remove ham and bone; cut any meat into small pieces. Work soup through sieve. Add diced ham and sherry. Season with salt and pepper to taste. If soup is too thick (it should be the consistency of heavy cream), stir in a little water. Heat through.

To serve, garnish with hard-cooked egg slices and thin lemon slices. Makes 6 servings.

BLACKBERRY — A purplish black, cone-shaped berry made up of many small fruits, each containing a small seed. Somewhat similar to dewberries, blackberries have been cultivated in America since the last half of the nineteenth century.

In ancient times, the fruit was important only for its supposed curative qualities. A syrup prepared from the berries was used medicinally. During this period the supply of berries seemed unlimited. In fact, some people considered the blackberry to be a nuisance and referred to the fruit as a weed. However, as with many other wild plants, the flavorful blackberry soon found its way into the kitchen. Its popularity increased as more uses were delegated to this once lowly berry.

How blackberries are grown: Although blackberries still grow wild in some areas, it is necessary to cultivate the fruit commercially to meet market demands. When picked, the ripe berry separates easily from the stem cap. Before maturity, the berries are either red or green.

Nutritional value: Blackberries contain some vitamins and minerals although they are not rich in any specific nutrient. One cup fresh berries yields 84 calories, while 1 cup canned berries packed in heavy syrup yields about 227 calories.

How to select: Fresh berries are in season from May through August. Select those which are plump, bright, clean, tender but not mushy, and of uniform color. Avoid those where leakage or staining is apparent on the container. Berries are also available canned or frozen.

How to store: Sort berries discarding soft or damaged fruit. Lightly cover unwashed berries and refrigerate. They can be refrigerated one to two days. For longer storage, they may be frozen.

How to use: Wash berries just before using. Serve fresh with sugar and cream, or add to fresh fruit cups or salads. Berries are used in jams, jellies, tarts, puddings, and pies. Wine is also made from the pressed berries. (See also *Berry*.)

Canned Blackberry Pie

      2 16-ounce cans blackberries
      3 tablespoons cornstarch
    ½ cup sugar
      1 tablespoon lemon juice
      1 tablespoon butter or margarine
         Plain Pastry for 2-crust 9-inch pie
         (See *Pastry*)

Drain berries, reserving 1½ cups syrup. In saucepan gradually add reserved syrup to cornstarch and ¼ teaspoon salt. Cook and stir over medium heat till bubbly. Stir in sugar; add lemon juice and butter. Fold in berries.

Divide pastry. Roll pastry to line 9-inch pie plate. Pour in filling. Roll remaining pastry. Adjust top crust; cut slits for escape of steam. Seal. Bake at 400° for 40 to 45 minutes.

Steamed Blackberry Pudding

    ½ cup butter or margarine
      1 cup sugar
      2 eggs
    ½ teaspoon vanilla
      2 cups sifted all-purpose flour
      3 teaspoons baking powder
    ½ teaspoon ground cinnamon
    ¾ cup milk
      2 tablespoons lemon juice
      1 16-ounce can blackberries
         Blackberry Sauce

Cream butter and sugar till light. Add eggs and vanilla; mix well. Sift together flour, baking powder, cinnamon, and ½ teaspoon salt. Add alternately with milk to creamed mixture, beating smooth after each addition. Stir in lemon juice. Drain berries, reserving syrup. Carefully fold in berries.

Pour into well-greased and floured 5½-cup mold. Cover with foil; tie with string. Place on rack in deep kettle. Add boiling water, 1 inch deep. Cover; steam 2 hours, adding water if needed. Cool 20 minutes; unmold. Slice and serve warm with sauce. Makes 8 servings.

Blackberry Sauce: Add water to reserved syrup to make 1½ cups. Mix ¼ cup sugar and 2 tablespoons cornstarch. Gradually stir in syrup. Cook and stir over medium heat till bubbly. Cook and stir 1 minute more. Stir in 1 tablespoon lemon juice. Makes 1⅔ cups.

Beaten egg whites lighten the pale yellow, rum-flavored custard of a Black Bottom Pie. The rich chocolate bottom layer helps create a tasty flavor duo for a memorable dessert.

BLACK-BOTTOM PIE—A lavish two-layered pie made of a custard-gelatin mixture, chocolate, and rum. Some versions use gingersnap-cookie crumbs for the crust in preference to a standard piecrust. The name originates from the dark bottom layer—a rich chocolate pudding.

Black Bottom Pie

Line 9-inch pie plate with Plain Pastry (See *Pastry*). Flute edge. Prick bottom and sides well with fork. Bake at 450° for 10 to 12 minutes or till golden; cool thoroughly.

Combine ½ cup sugar and 1 tablespoon cornstarch. Slowly add 2 cups milk, scalded, to 4 beaten egg yolks. Stir in sugar mixture. Cook and stir till custard thickens and coats spoon. Remove from heat; add 1 teaspoon vanilla.

To *1 cup* of the custard, add one 6-ounce package semisweet chocolate pieces (1 cup). Stir till melted. Pour into pastry shell; chill.

Soften 1 envelope unflavored gelatin (1 tablespoon) in ¼ cup cold water; add to remaining *hot* custard. Stir till dissolved. Stir in ½ teaspoon rum extract *or* 2 tablespoons light rum. Chill till slightly thickened.

Beat 4 egg whites till soft peaks form. Gradually add ½ cup sugar; beat till stiff peaks form. Fold in gelatin-custard mixture. Chill, if necessary, till mixture mounds when spooned. Pile over chocolate layer; chill till firm. Garnish with shaved semisweet chocolate and bias-cut banana slices.

BLACK CURRANT—A tart, black berry of the currant family. In Europe where they are prevalent, black currants are used in jams and jellies or as the base for a sweet-flavored wine and liqueur both of which are called cassis. (See also *Currant*.)

BLACK DRIED MUSHROOM—A savory oriental mushroom with meatlike texture. Of the two varieties, one is a dark brownish color; the other is thick and flower-shaped. Both types can be used interchangeably.

To prepare for use, pour boiling water over the mushrooms. Allow them to soak at least 15 minutes; squeeze to remove excess water before slicing. The strongly flavored soaking water can be used as a mushroom stock in meat casseroles, if desired.

Succulent black mushrooms are adaptable to many Oriental dishes but should be used sparingly. (See *Mushroom, Oriental Cookery* for additional information.)

BLACK-EYED PEA—An oval-shaped bean also known as cowpea, identified by its black spot or "eye." These peas are usually cooked with salt pork, fatback, or bacon. Black-eyed peas are commonly used in many parts of the world, particularly Africa and India. In the southern United States these good-luck beans traditionally are served on New Year's Day in a dish called Hopping John. This recipe received its name either from the energetic waiter who served the dish or from the children who danced around the table before the food was served. (See *Bean, Regional Cookery* for additional information.)

Hopping John

> 1 **pound dried black-eyed**
> **peas (2 cups)**
> 1 **medium ham hock**
> 1 **16-ounce can tomatoes, cut up**
> 1 **cup chopped onion**
> 1 **cup chopped celery**
> 1 **whole bay leaf**
> 1 **cup uncooked long-grain rice**

Rinse peas; add to 8 cups cold water. Bring to boiling. Simmer 2 minutes then remove from heat. Cover; let stand 1 hour (or soak overnight). Drain. Combine peas, ham hock, 4 cups water, tomatoes, onion, celery, 1 tablespoon salt, bay leaf, and dash pepper in Dutch oven.

Cover and simmer till peas are *almost* tender, about 1¼ hours. Add rice; cook 40 minutes. Add more water, if needed. Lift out ham hock; remove bone and mince meat. Add ham to pea mixture. Remove bay leaf. Serves 12 to 15.

BLACK PEPPER—A hot, pungent spice, the fruit of the *Piper nigrum*. The partially ripened red berries are dried for use. In drying, the outer shell changes from red to almost black, but the inside remains white.

In market black pepper can be bought whole as peppercorns or ground in regular, medium, or coarse (cracked) mill. (See *Pepper, Spice* for additional information.)

BLACKSTRAP MOLASSES—A bitterly flavored thick, black syrup, resulting from the liquid obtained from the last boiling of sugar cane in the production of sugar.

Blackstrap contains all the gum, ash, and indigestible matter present in unprocessed crude sugar. It is not as high nutritionally as lighter molasses. (See *Molasses, Sugar* for additional information.)

BLACK WALNUT—A two-lobed nut, also called Persian walnut, enclosed in an extremely hard, rough, dark shell. The nutmeat is oily, rich, and distinctive in flavor.

Because of the hard shell, black walnuts are usually sold shelled. Nuts in the shell are available only where these trees flourish. (See also *Walnut*.)

BLANCH—To precook briefly in boiling water or steam. Blanching serves several functions. After just a few seconds of blanching the skins of foods like peaches and tomatoes can be removed easily. Fruits and vegetables are blanched before freezing to stop enzyme action. This prevents spoilage during storage and helps foods retain their natural color and flavor.

This process can also help to whiten sweetbreads or to decrease the pungency and flavor strength of strong-flavored vegetables such as shallots and onions. (See also *Freezing*.)

BLANCMANGE *(bluh mânj')*—A delicate, white milk pudding usually shaped in a mold. The French developed Blancmange, originally a jelly, into a dessert during the 1600s. The cold pudding was traditionally thickened with ground almonds, set with gelatin, and flavored with rum or *kirchwasser*. Today's recipes often substitute cornstarch, flour, or Irish moss for the almonds. (See also *French Cookery.*)

Blancmange

⅓ cup sugar
3 tablespoons cornstarch
2½ cups milk
1½ teaspoons vanilla

Mix sugar, cornstarch, and ¼ teaspoon salt in saucepan; gradually blend in milk. Cook over medium heat, stirring constantly, till mixture thickens. Cook 2 or 3 minutes more. Add vanilla. Pour into sherbets; chill. Or pour into individual molds rinsed with cold water; chill till firm. Unmold to serve. Makes 5 or 6 servings.

BLAND—A term used to describe food that is smooth, unseasoned, or dull in flavor, and does not stimulate the taste senses.

BLANQUETTE *(blân ket')*—A French stew of chicken, veal, or lamb cooked in a creamy white sauce usually thickened with egg yolk and slightly acidified with lemon juice. Onions and mushrooms are often added. (See also *French Cookery.*)

BLARNEY CHEESE—An Irish cheese with large holes like Swiss and covered with an Edam-like red paraffin rind. It has a distinctive flavor suitable for appetizers, main dishes, and desserts. (See also *Cheese.*)

Sold cut
in wedges,
Blarney Cheese.

BLAZER PAN—The cooking pan of a standard chafing dish. (See also *Chafing Dish.*)

BLEND—To mix two or more ingredients together thoroughly until smooth and uniform in texture, flavor, and color. This action may be accomplished with a spoon, rotary beater, electric mixer, or blender.

BLENDER—A portable electric appliance with small rotating blades that blend, chop, or liquefy. Although invented nearly 40 years ago solely as a drink mixer, the blender is now used to perform assorted tasks of food preparation.

A blender consists of two main parts: the base which houses the motor and the blender container with cutting blades. When in motion, these blades rotate at an extremely high rate of speed (thousands of revolutions per second), to transform the mixture into the desired state.

How to select: Choose a blender according to the qualities that make it a useful appliance. The base should be sturdy and well-balanced to avoid tipping or excessive vibrating. The motor should be rated with a high wattage so that blending is possible at high and low speeds.

Many blender models offer a range of speeds to suit specific blending jobs. These may be regulated with lever controls, push buttons, or a timer dial. Solid state controls are available, too, on some models.

Blender containers are usually made of transparent materials such as glass or heat-resistant plastic which give the homemaker a clear view of the mixture being blended. A smooth interior surface will assure the container will be easy to wash after use. Since the cover should fit snugly in place during operation, a removable cap in the center facilitates adding foods while the blender is operating.

To make the blender convenient for small chopping jobs, most models will accommodate a mason jar or specially designed small container which doubles for food storage when blending is completed.

How to use: The blender does easily and quickly many drudgery jobs such as puréeing, chopping, and mixing. By regulating blender speed and blending time, an assortment of foods ranging from smooth soups to chopped nuts is achieved.

Perhaps the blender's chief use is in the preparation of liquefied foods and drinks. Sometimes the beverage will be frosty fruit punch or a favorite cocktail. Another day the choice will be a thick soda or milk shake. Most beverages involve a two-step mixing and aerating procedure. The first blending is at low speed followed by a few seconds at high setting. Using a blender when diluting frozen juice concentrates aerates and gives the drink flavor more nearly like freshly squeezed juice.

When liquefying food, some water, milk, or fruit juice is blended with the cut-up food and whirled into a smooth mixture.

Strawberry Frosted Soda

  1 3-ounce package strawberry-
      flavored gelatin
  1 quart cold milk
  1 quart strawberry ice cream

Blending tips

• Read the instruction booklet to become familiar with the blender's advantages.

• Follow recipe directions exactly. Because the blades turn so fast, most blending operations require seconds rather than minutes.

• Avoid overloading container. Thin- or medium-consistency liquids can fill the container three-fourths full; thick liquids, halfway. When grating or crushing, blend one cup of product at a time. Blend one-half cup fibrous foods, like cooked meat, at a time.

• When liquids are blended, put enough in the container to cover the blades.

• Use a long, slim rubber spatula to scrape sides, remembering to scrape *after* the motor has been turned off.

• Coarsely dice solid foods before blending.

Place 1 cup boiling water and gelatin in blender container; cover and blend till gelatin is completely dissolved. Pour ½ *cup* of the gelatin mixture into a measuring cup; set aside. Add *half* the cold milk to the remaining gelatin mixture in blender container; blend on low speed till mixture is well blended.

Add *half* the strawberry ice cream; cover and blend just till mixture is smooth. Pour soda into tall glasses. Repeat with reserved gelatin mixture, milk, and strawberry ice cream. Garnish each glass with a whole fresh strawberry, if desired. Makes 6 servings.

Have an aversion for chopping nuts, grating cheese or chocolate, or making crumbs from bread or crackers? The blender will zip through these tasks in a hurry, too. Put about one cup of the coarsely diced food in the blender container. Then just cover and blend a few seconds.

Or, make the most delicious coleslaw instantly from raw vegetables. Loosely fill the blender container with the coarsely diced food. Pour in just enough water to cover the vegetables. Cover; blend a few seconds, drain well, and mix with a favorite salad dressing just before serving.

Whole vanilla wafers provide the crust for Pink Parfait Pie—another blender wonder. Top with whipped cream and berries.

Blenders are also efficient for blending thin batters as popovers, pancakes, and waffles; homogenizing mixtures for salad dressings, sauces, gravies, and soups; or puréeing, a technique ideal for preparing baby foods, fluffy salads, and airy desserts.

Giant Pecan Popovers

  ¼ cup pecans
  1 cup milk
  2 eggs
  1 cup sifted all-purpose flour
  ¼ teaspoon salt

Chop pecans in blender container; empty and set nuts aside. Place milk and eggs in blender container; cover and blend 2 seconds. Add flour and salt; cover and blend 10 seconds. Stir in pecans. Fill well-greased custard cups half full. Bake at 475° for 15 minutes.

Reduce heat to 350°; bake 25 to 30 minutes longer or till brown and firm. A few minutes before removing from oven, prick each popover with a fork to let steam escape. If you like popovers dry and crisp, turn off oven and leave popovers in oven 30 minutes with door ajar. Serve hot. Makes 6 to 8.

Because the blades turn so rapidly, the blender may not effectively incorporate air into egg whites for meringue. Also, liquid ingredients are essential for a smooth operation and kneading stiff doughs or grinding raw meat can overtax cutting blades and motor. Likewise, check instruction book before attempting to crush ice. A special attachment may be necessary.

Cottage Cheese Fluff

  1 cup dry cottage cheese
    Non-caloric liquid sweetener
      equal to 2 tablespoons sugar
  4 teaspoons lemon juice
  ½ cup skim milk

In blender container combine cottage cheese, sweetener, and lemon juice; blend till creamy. Add milk, a tablespoon at a time, till of desired consistency. Serve with lettuce. Makes 1 cup.

Blender Pots de Crème

  ¼ cup cold water
  1½ tablespoons unflavored gelatin
  2 teaspoons instant coffee powder
  ½ cup hot milk
        . . .
  1 6-ounce package semisweet
      chocolate pieces (1 cup)
  1 tablespoon sugar
  ½ teaspoon vanilla
    Dash salt
        . . .
  1¼ cups *drained* finely crushed ice
  2 egg yolks
  1 cup whipping cream

Add cold water, gelatin, and coffee powder to blender container. Cover; blend few seconds on low speed. Add milk; blend till gelatin is dissolved. Add chocolate, sugar, vanilla, and dash salt. Cover; blend just till smooth. Add ice and yolks; blend till smooth. While blender is running, add cream. Blend 20 seconds or till it *begins* to thicken. Pour into small sherbets. Chill 10 minutes. Makes 5 or 6 servings.

Pink Parfait Pie

Pour ¾ cup boiling water in blender container; add one 3-ounce package strawberry-flavored gelatin. Let stand 10 seconds to soften. Cover; blend 10 seconds or till gelatin is dissolved.

Cut one 10-ounce package frozen sliced strawberries in half. Thaw *half* for topping. Add remaining half to gelatin mixture with 1 pint strawberry ice cream. Blend till smooth, about 20 seconds. Chill the mixture about 5 to 10 minutes, stirring occasionally until it begins to hold a mound easily.

Pile filling into one 8-inch baked pastry shell *or* one 8-inch whole vanilla wafer crust. (See *Pastry* or *Vanilla Wafer* for recipes.) Chill pie till firm. Garnish with whipped cream and remaining strawberries. Makes 6 servings.

Creamy, full-flavored spread

Let the blender prepare Shrimp-Dill Pâté. →
To assure having pieces of shrimp throughout, blend shrimp only a few seconds.

The flavors of sunny apricots and tangy oranges meld in this tantalizing blender salad entitled Orange-Apricot Ring.

Orange-Apricot Ring

Drain one 16-ounce can apricot halves, reserving syrup. Purée apricots in blender. Add enough water to syrup to make 1½ cups. Combine syrup, two 3-ounce packages orange-flavored gelatin, and dash salt; heat to boiling, stirring till dissolved. Remove from heat.

Add one 6-ounce can frozen orange juice concentrate; stir till melted. Add purée and 1 cup cold water. Pour into 5½-cup ring mold. Chill till firm. Unmold; garnish with lettuce, orange sections, and frosted grapes. Serves 8 to 10.

Grating, chopping, and crushing are three duties the blender does well; but special care must be taken not to over-blend. Be sure solid foods are first coarsely diced. One- or two-second blends are sufficient for a coarse chop; a few seconds longer for a fine chop. Often water to cover is added to vegetables for better chopping; the food is then well drained.

Speedy Salsa

Cut ½ medium onion and 1 medium stalk celery in pieces; put in blender container with 1½ canned green chilies, 2 tablespoons red wine vinegar, 1 tablespoon salad oil, 1 teaspoon *each* salt and coriander seed. Blend at low speed till vegetables are finely chopped, stopping and starting motor several times, if necessary. Turn onion mixture into bowl.

Quarter 4 ripe medium tomatoes; discard seeds. Put in blender; cover and blend at low speed, stopping and starting motor several times, till chopped (a few seconds). Drain tomatoes well; mix with onion mixture, 1 tablespoon mustard seed, and dash pepper. Chill thoroughly. Makes 3 cups relish.

Shrimp-Dill Pâté

- 1½ cups tomato juice
- 2 envelopes unflavored gelatin (2 tablespoons)

• • •

- 2 cups dairy sour cream
- 1 tablespoon dried dillweed
- 2 tablespoons lemon juice
- ½ teaspoon salt
- ½ teaspoon Worcestershire sauce
- 1 4½- or 5-ounce can shrimp, drained (about ¾ cup)

Add ½ *cup* tomato juice and gelatin to blender container. Cover; blend on low till gelatin is softened. Bring remaining tomato juice to boil; add to blender container. Blend on low till gelatin is dissolved in tomato juice.

Turn blender to high; add remaining ingredients *except* shrimp. Blend till smooth. Stop blender; add shrimp. Turn blender on and off quickly several times till shrimp are chopped. Pour into 5½-cup mold. Chill till firm.

Blender Potato Pancakes

Put 4 eggs in blender container; cover and blend till fluffy, about 5 seconds. In order given add ⅔ cup sifted all-purpose flour; 1½ teaspoons salt; 2 tablespoons salad oil; ½ cup milk; ½ small onion; 2 cups diced, peeled raw potatoes; and 1 teaspoon ascorbic acid color keeper. Blend 5 seconds or till potatoes are finely grated—not lumpy.

Using about 2 tablespoons batter for each pancake, bake on hot greased griddle about 2 minutes on a side. Turn once. Do not stack cakes. Serve with hot applesauce. Makes 30.

BLEU CHEESE—The French term for blue-veined, mold-ripened cheese manufactured in France. In the United States the term often refers to any imported blue-veined cheese. (See *Blue Cheese, Roquefort Cheese* for additional information.)

BLIN—A small, quite delicate, Russian and Central European pancake made with buckwheat flour and leavened with yeast. Customarily served during Shrovetide, the three days immediately preceding Lent, blini are accompanied by caviar, cheese, or sour cream. (See also *Russian Cookery.*)

BLINTZE *(blint' suh)*—A thin, rolled pancake filled with cottage cheese, fruit, or meat and served with sour cream, applesauce or fruit jam. The blintze resembles a small oblong pancake with tucked-in ends.

Blintzes, adaptations of Russian blini, are a popular Jewish food specialty. They may be served for the main or dessert course. (See also *Jewish Cookery.*)

Israeli Cheese Blintzes

Mix ¾ cup sifted all-purpose flour *or* ½ cup matzo meal (cake meal) and ½ teaspoon salt. Combine 1 cup milk and 2 slightly beaten eggs; gradually add to flour, beating till smooth. Pour about 2 tablespoons batter into hot, lightly greased 6-inch skillet; quickly swirl pan to spread batter evenly. Cook over medium heat till golden on bottom and edges begin to pull away from side, about 2 minutes. Loosen; turn out of skillet. Repeat.

Blend together 1½ cups well-drained cream-style cottage cheese, 1 slightly beaten egg, 2 tablespoons sugar, ½ teaspoon vanilla, and dash ground cinnamon. Place pancakes cooked side up; spoon some filling in center of each. Overlap sides atop filling, then overlap ends.

Brown on both sides in small amount of hot shortening. Serve hot, topped with sour cream and cherry preserves. Makes 6 or 7 servings.

BLITZ TORTE—A dessert confection of cake and meringuelike topping baked together. A filling is usually spread between the layers; then the cake is garnished richly with nuts. (See also *Torte.*)

Mocha Blitz Torte

  1 package 2-layer-size chocolate
     cake mix
  1 tablespoon instant coffee
     powder
      • • •
  1 package fluffy white frosting
     mix (for 2-layer cake)
 ⅔ cup slivered almonds
  1 2-ounce package dessert
     topping mix

Prepare cake mix following package directions, adding coffee powder to batter. Pour into 2 greased and paper-lined 9-inch round cake pans. Bake at 350° for 20 minutes.

Meanwhile, prepare frosting mix following package directions. Remove cake layers from oven; quickly spread frosting over tops, keeping it from touching cake pans. Sprinkle each layer with *half* the almonds. Return to oven and bake 15 minutes more.

Cool layers in pans. (Frosting will settle somewhat as cake cools.) Remove cake from pans. Prepare dessert topping mix following package directions. Place one cake layer on plate, frosting side up; spread with topping. Top with second layer; chill cake.

Mocha Blitz Torte, the modern version of a well-known dessert, starts with a chocolate cake mix and a fluffy white frosting mix.

BLOATER—A large, fat member of the herring family that is lightly salted and smoked before marketing. The fish may be split and broiled or panfried. They are often poached in water and served with a bit of melted butter. A bloater paste to use in a sandwich spread of salad dressing is prepared by sieving the poached fish and blending it into creamed butter. Bloaters are a favorite national English breakfast dish. (See also *Herring.*)

BLOND *(blon)*—A French term describing the faintly creamy, off-white color of a roux used to thicken sauces and gravies. (See also *Roux.*)

BLOOD ORANGE—A variety of the sweet orange identified by the deep red color of the delicious pulp and juice. It is one of the lesser-known oranges grown in the Western states. They are available from mid-March to mid-May. (See also *Orange.*)

BLOOD PUDDING—A large, dark sausage made with pig's blood and suet. It is also known as blood sausage or black pudding. Under the latter name it is a traditional French dish served at supper following the Christmas midnight mass.

A type of blood sausage was familiar in early Assyrian and Greek times. The dish continues to be popular throughout Europe and Asia, but except in national or ethnic communities has never achieved widespread acceptance in the United States. Although blood pudding is generally made with pig's blood, beef blood is used in some of the commercial sausages available. (See also *Sausage.*)

BLUEBERRY—The name given in North America to the fruit and the shrubs of a certain member of the heath family. They range in color from purplish blue to almost black. The sweet, edible berries are known by different names in different geographic locations. The British, for example, call them whortleberries or bilberries.

Many Americans incorrectly regard the names blueberry and huckleberry as interchangeable. Actually, blueberries have many tiny seeds while huckleberries contain ten rather large, hard seeds. The reason for this confusion is really very simple. Some of the large, plump commercial blueberries are a horticultural development of the wild, swamp huckleberry which grew along cranberry bogs.

The daughter of a pioneer cranberry grower believed that if you could cultivate the cranberry, certainly the huckleberry could be cultivated, too. With the cooperation of the U.S. Department of Agriculture she set out to develop a berry which would be uniform, full flavored, and true-blue in color. Success did not come immediately but the luscious, giant blueberries which come to market today are a tribute to her vision and the hard work required to develop a new fruit variety.

Blueberries grow singly or in clusters depending on the species. There is diversity in bush size, too. Low bush plants grow from 6 to 18 inches high. The tall, highbush varieties measure 10 to 15 feet. Some of the wild berries are tiny when compared to the large, cultivated varieties.

Blueberries are native to many climates. Although they are known above the Arctic Circle and in the swampy regions of Florida, most of the cultivated berries for the North American market come from North Carolina, New Jersey, and Michigan.

Nutritional Value: Blueberries contain 87 calories per cup. They have small amounts of vitamins A and C plus some of the B group, thiamine and riboflavin.

How to select: When buying blueberries look for a dark blue color with a soft powdery bloom. This silvery bloom is a natural, protective waxy coating. The berries should be plump and fresh looking, fairly uniform in size and free from stem or leaves. Blueberries begin coming to market at the end of May. While fresh berries are at peak supply during June, July, and August with some available in September, frozen and canned berries and pie filling are available in supermarkets year-round.

How to store: Like all members of the berry family, blueberries are perishable and should be used soon after purchase. They should be stored in a covered container in the refrigerator and washed just before use.

How to use: Beautiful blues are delicious by the bowlful with milk or cream and sugar or topped with a dollop of sour cream and a sprinkling of brown sugar. Likewise, a cascade of berries will enhance breakfast cereal or a luncheon salad plate. Muffins, quick breads, and shortcakes are popular uses for the fruit. And, who can pass up a juicy wedge of blueberry pie?

Blueberries freeze satisfactorily with syrup or sugar pack. Some homemakers prefer to pack them without the addition of sweetening. Plans for final use will determine which is the most convenient method of packaging. (See also *Berries.*)

Blueberry-Lemon Muffins

    1¾ cups sifted all-purpose flour
    ¼ cup sugar
    2½ teaspoons baking powder
    ¾ teaspoon salt
    ¾ cup milk
    1 well-beaten egg
    ⅓ cup salad oil
    1 cup fresh blueberries *or* 1 cup
        frozen whole blueberries,
        thawed
    2 tablespoons sugar
    1 teaspoon grated lemon peel
        Butter or margarine, melted
        Sugar

Sift together flour, the ¼ cup sugar, baking powder, and salt into mixing bowl. Make a well in center of flour mixture. Combine milk, egg, and oil. Add all at once to dry ingredients. Stir quickly, just till moistened.

Toss together blueberries and the 2 tablespoons sugar; gently stir into batter along with lemon peel. Fill greased 2½-inch muffin pans ⅔ full. Bake at 400° for about 25 minutes. While muffins are still warm, dip tops in melted butter or margarine then in a little sugar. Serve immediately. Makes 12 muffins.

When blueberries are plentiful

Take full advantage of the goodness of fresh blueberries and bake sugar-crusted Blueberry-Lemon Muffins for breakfast.

Blueberry Buckle

½ cup shortening
¾ cup sugar
1 well-beaten egg
2 cups sifted all-purpose flour
2½ teaspoons baking powder
¼ teaspoon salt
½ cup milk
2 cups fresh blueberries
    Cinnamon Crumbs

Cream shortening and sugar. Add egg; beat till fluffy. Sift flour, baking powder, and salt together; add alternately with milk. Spread in greased 11x7x1½-inch pan. Top with blueberries. Sprinkle Cinnamon Crumbs atop. Bake at 350° about 45 minutes. Cut in squares. Serve warm with cream, if desired. Serves 8 to 10.

Cinnamon Crumbs: Mix ½ cup *each* sugar, sifted all-purpose flour, and ½ teaspoon ground cinnamon. Cut in ¼ cup butter till crumbly.

Blueberry Shortcake

2 cups sifted all-purpose flour
2 tablespoons sugar
2½ teaspoons baking powder
½ teaspoon salt
½ cup butter or margarine
1 slightly beaten egg
½ cup milk
1 cup fresh blueberries
2 teaspoons sugar
    Blueberry Sauce

Sift together flour, 2 tablespoons sugar, baking powder, and salt; cut in butter. Combine egg and milk; stir into flour mixture. Divide dough in half. Gently pat *half* into greased 8x1½-inch round cake pan. Top with blueberries.

On waxed paper, roll remaining dough to an 8-inch circle. Invert and fit dough over blueberries. Remove paper; sprinkle dough with 2 teaspoons sugar. Bake at 400° for 25 to 30 minutes. Cut shortcake into 6 wedges.

Serve with warm *Blueberry Sauce:* In saucepan combine ¼ cup sugar and 1½ tablespoons cornstarch; blend in 1 cup cold water. Cook and stir till mixture is thickened and bubbly. Add 1 cup fresh blueberries; cook 3 minutes. Remove from heat; stir in 1 tablespoon lemon juice and ¼ cup butter or margarine. Serves 6.

Blueberry Pie

Prepare pastry for 2-crust 9-inch pie. (See *Pastry.*) Line pie plate with bottom crust. Mix 4 cups fresh blueberries, ¾ to 1 cup sugar, 3 tablespoons all-purpose flour, ½ teaspoon grated lemon peel, ½ teaspoon *each* ground cinnamon and ground nutmeg, and dash salt. Fill pie shell. Drizzle with 1 to 2 tablespoons lemon juice; dot with 1 tablespoon butter. Cut slits in top crust. Cover filling; seal. Bake at 400° for 35 to 40 minutes.

Blueberry Strata Pie

1 16-ounce can blueberries
1 8¾-ounce can crushed pineapple
1 8-ounce package cream
    cheese, softened
3 tablespoons sugar
1 tablespoon milk
½ teaspoon vanilla
1 9-inch *baked* pastry shell,
    cooled (See *Pastry.*)
¼ cup sugar
2 tablespoons cornstarch
1 teaspoon lemon juice
½ cup whipping cream

Drain fruits; reserving syrups. Blend cheese and next 3 ingredients. Reserving 2 tablespoons pineapple, stir remaining into cheese mixture. Spread over pastry shell; chill. Blend ¼ cup sugar, cornstarch, and ¼ teaspoon salt. Combine reserved syrups; measure 1½ cups. Blend into cornstarch mixture. Cook and stir till bubbly. Stir in blueberries and lemon juice; cool. Pour over cheese layer; chill. Top with whipped cream and reserved pineapple.

Blueberry Cream Salad

Dissolve one 3-ounce package lemon-flavored gelatin in 1 cup boiling water; cool. Stir in one 21-ounce can blueberry pie filling and 2 tablespoons lemon juice. Chill till partially set. Spoon *half* the mixture into 8½x4½x2½-inch loaf dish. Chill till *almost* firm. (Keep remaining gelatin at room temperature.) Combine ½ cup dairy sour cream and 1 tablespoon sugar. Spread over *almost* firm gelatin. Top with remaining gelatin. Chill till firm. Serves 6 to 8.

BLUE CHEESE—Technically, any of the blue-veined cheeses, but in American markets blue generally refers to domestic and *bleu* to imported varieties. The cheese is creamy white with distinctive bluish-green veins. It is semisoft in texture and crumbles rather easily. Blue cheese has a piquant, salt and pepper flavor.

Classical references seem to indicate that some forms of blue cheese were known in pre-Christian times. A shepherd boy's lunch lost in a cave started the blue-cheese making industry in France according to a popular legend. When he found the cheese, it was streaked with mold but delicious. In 1411 Charles VI set the boundaries of Roquefort in France for blue cheeses that could legally bear that name. Thus Roquefort is a blue cheese, but only blue cheeses meeting certain legal specifications can be designated as Roquefort cheese.

The history of blue cheese making in America is relatively short. First attempts to produce the cheese took place about 1918. However, since the flavor and blue veining or mold comes from *Penicillium roqueforti*, production was not practical until after the blue mold was isolated and became available commercially.

How blue cheese is produced: Almost all American blue cheese is made from cow's milk although a process has been developed for using goat's milk. The type of milk used is one of the important differences between the American varieties and French Roquefort which by law must be made only from ewe's milk.

The blue mold powder which generates the flavor streaks is added at one of several points during the cheese making. Some producers combine it with the milk; others stir it into the curd, while still others sprinkle the powder over the curd as it drains in large perforated cylinders called hoops. Once drained and formed into wheels, the cheese is salted, and the wheels are pierced deeply to allow the gas of fermentation to escape and air to enter. The air is necessary in order to promote growth of the flavorful mold throughout the cheese.

All Roquefort cheese is ripened according to traditional procedures in the limestone caves found in the area. Some

Blue-veined blue cheese with fruit.

American blue cheeses are ripened in similar caves of sandstone. Other cheeses are aged commercially under carefully controlled conditions where temperature and humidity simulate that of the caves. A minimum curing time of two months is necessary to develop flavor and texture. Among cheese makers there are a number who prefer to age their blue cheese for longer periods of time.

At last the wheels of cheese are ready for marketing. In specialty cheese shops the big wheels are cut to the customer's order. The supermarket shopper will find blue cheese in foil-wrapped portions in the dairy case. Because of the growing popularity of blue cheese, it is an important ingredient in many tempting commercially-prepared dips, spreads, and salad dressings, and food specialties.

Nutritional value: A one-ounce portion of blue cheese contains 103 calories. It also provides protein, calcium, vitamin A, and the B vitamin, riboflavin.

How to store: Cover cut surfaces of blue cheese tightly with foil or clear plastic wrap. Properly wrapped, it will keep several weeks in the refrigerator or freezer.

How to serve: Wedges of blue cheese with fresh apples or pears will always be popular for dessert. Because it goes so well with fruit and vegetables, many salad or sauce combinations are possible. Blue cheese also appears in dips for crackers or in appetizing tidbits. It brings elegance when crumbled over steak or blended into a hamburger mixture before broiling the meat patties. (See also *Cheese.*)

Blue Cheese Bites

> 1 package refrigerated biscuits
>   (10 biscuits)
> ¼ cup butter
> 3 tablespoons crumbled blue
>   cheese

Cut biscuits into quarters; arrange pieces evenly in two 8-inch round baking dishes. Melt the butter and blue cheese together. Pour mixture over biscuit pieces, coating well. Bake at 400° for 12 to 15 minutes, or till golden brown. Serve hot. Makes 40 appetizers.

Clam-Cheese Dip

Combine one 8-ounce package cream cheese, softened; 2 ounces crumbled blue cheese (½ cup); 1 tablespoon snipped chives *or* green onion tops; ¼ teaspoon salt; and bottled hot pepper sauce to taste. Beat until smooth.

Drain one 7½-ounce can minced clams, reserving liquor. Stir clams into cheese mixture. Add enough reserved clam liquor (*or* milk) to make of spreading consistency. Keep chilled; remove from refrigerator 15 minutes before serving. Pass crackers or chips. Makes 1⅔ cups.

Blue Cheese Salad Bowl

> 1 small head cauliflower
> ½ cup onion rings
> ¼ cup sliced pimiento-stuffed
>   green olives
> ⅔ cup clear French salad dressing
>   with herbs and spices
> 2 ounces blue cheese, crumbled
> 1 head lettuce, torn in pieces

Separate cauliflower into flowerets; slice. Add to onion rings and olives. Marinate in dressing ½ hour in refrigerator. Add blue cheese and lettuce. Toss. Makes 8 servings.

Refreshing Frosted Cheese Mold

← How cool can a salad be? The creamy ring gets its flavor from blue cheese. It is filled with frosted grapes, fruits, and fresh mint.

Frosted Cheese Mold

> 1 cup milk
> 2 envelopes unflavored gelatin
>   (2 tablespoons)
> 2 12-ounce cartons cream-style
>   cottage cheese (3 cups)
> 2 ounces blue cheese, crumbled
> 1 6-ounce can frozen limeade
>   concentrate, thawed
> ½ cup broken pecans, toasted
>   and salted
> 6 drops green food coloring
> 1 cup whipping cream
>   Frosted grapes
>   Mint sprigs
>   Lime wedges

Pour milk into large saucepan. Sprinkle gelatin over milk to soften. Place over low heat and stir till gelatin is dissolved. Remove from heat.

Beat cottage cheese and blue cheese together till well blended; stir into gelatin mixture. Add concentrate, pecans, and food coloring. Whip cream; fold into gelatin mixture. Turn into 6½-cup ring mold and chill 4 to 6 hours. Unmold on serving plate; fill center with melon balls and orange sections, if desired. Garnish with frosted grapes and mint sprigs. Pass lime wedges. Makes 10 to 12 servings.

Note: To frost grapes, brush with lightly beaten egg white. Sprinkle with sugar.

Blue Cheese-Spud Salad

> 5 cups cubed, peeled, cooked
>   potatoes
> 1 cup chopped celery
> 4 hard-cooked eggs, chopped
> ½ cup sliced green onion
> ¼ cup chopped green pepper
> 1 cup dairy sour cream
> ⅓ cup evaporated milk
> 1 ounce blue cheese, crumbled
>   (¼ cup)
> 2 tablespoons vinegar
> ¼ teaspoon dry mustard

Sprinkle cooked potatoes with 1 teaspoon salt. Combine potatoes, celery, eggs, onion, and green pepper. Blend together remaining ingredients and ⅛ teaspoon pepper. Pour over potato mixture; toss lightly. Chill. Serves 10 to 12.

Blue Cheese Fruit Cups

      1 16-ounce can fruit cocktail
      2 envelopes unflavored gelatin
         (2 tablespoons)
      2 cups orange juice
      1 3-ounce package cream cheese,
         cubed and softened
    ½ cup mayonnaise or salad
         dressing
    ¼ cup lemon juice
      2 tablespoons sugar
      1 ounce blue cheese, crumbled
         (¼ cup)
    ½ cup broken pecans

Drain fruit cocktail, reserving 1 cup syrup. Soften gelatin in *half* the reserved syrup. Heat orange juice just to boiling and add to softened gelatin, stirring till gelatin dissolves. Slowly add hot mixture to cream cheese, beating with rotary beater till smooth.

Add remaining reserved fruit syrup, mayonnaise, lemon juice, sugar, and dash salt. Beat gelatin mixture again till smooth. Chill till partially set. Stir in drained fruit cocktail, blue cheese, and nuts. Spoon into ten ½-cup molds. Chill till firm. Serves 10.

Zippy Blue Cheese Sauce

In saucepan melt 2 tablespoons butter or margarine. Blend in 2 tablespoons all-purpose flour. Add 1 cup milk and 1 chicken bouillon cube. Cook and stir till mixture thickens and bubbles. Remove from heat. Stir in ¼ cup dairy sour cream and 1 ounce blue cheese, crumbled (¼ cup). Heat through; do not boil. Serve with vegetables. Makes 1¼ cups.

Blue Cheese Dogs

Combine ⅓ cup dairy sour cream; 1 ounce blue cheese, crumbled (¼ cup); ¼ cup sweet pickle relish; 2 tablespoons instant minced onion; and 2 tablespoons prepared mustard.

Spread 2 tablespoons cheese mixture on each of 8 split and toasted frankfurter buns. Insert a frankfurter into each bun. Wrap buns in heavy foil; heat in 400° oven or on grill over *medium* coals for about 10 minutes or until frankfurter is heated through. Makes 8 servings.

Blue Cheese Burgers

    ⅓ cup chopped onion
    ⅓ cup crumbled blue cheese
      1 tablespoon Worcestershire sauce
      2 teaspoons salt
      2 pounds ground beef
           • • •
      1 unsliced loaf French bread
    ½ cup butter, softened
    ¼ cup prepared mustard

Combine onion, blue cheese, Worcestershire sauce, and salt. Add meat; mix well. Shape mixture into 10 oval patties slightly larger than diameter of French loaf. Cut French loaf in twenty ½-inch slices (freeze any extra bread). Blend butter and mustard; spread on one side of each bread slice. Reassemble loaf, placing buttered sides together. Wrap in heavy foil; place on grill for 15 minutes. Broil burgers about 8 minutes; turn and broil 4 to 7 minutes. Serve between French bread slices. Serves 10.

BLUE CRAB—One of the principal types of crab found along the Atlantic and Gulf Coasts. Blue crabs have a brownish green or dark green shell and blue claws. Adults measure five to seven inches across the shell and weigh one-fourth to one pound.

Blue crabs are available in the market in the hard-shell and soft-shell stages. (Soft-shell crabs have shed the shell and not yet grown another.) The consumer can purchase live crabs, crabs cooked in the shell, cooked meat picked from the shell, or pasteurized cooked meat packed in cans. Few are frozen. (See also *Crab.*)

BLUEFISH—A blue and silver, oily fish also called skipjack and related to the pompano. It is found in East Coast waters. The one and one-half to two-pound size when filleted is delicious broiled. Larger bluefish weighing up to 6 or 7 pounds are often stuffed and baked. (See also *Fish.*)

BLUEGILL—A Midwestern freshwater fish of the sunfish family. The meat is firm and flaky, its flavor pleasing. The fish is small, rarely over one pound in weight. It is generally prepared either by broiling quickly or panfrying. (See also *Fish.*)

BLUEPOINT—A small oyster that is the appropriate size to serve on the half shell. Blue Point once referred to only the oysters caught at Great South Bay, Long Island. Now, however, it applies to those from the Atlantic and Gulf Coasts of this particular size. (See also *Oyster*.)

BODY—A term used to describe the satisfying feel of a food on the tongue. It also describes the depth and richness of flavor in a wine that leaves a pleasant lasting impression on the palate.

BOIL—To cook food in liquid or maintain liquid at a temperature at which bubbles rise to the surface and break. The boiling point is the moment during heating a liquid when bubbling begins and the whole mass of liquid begins to move. At sea level water boils at 212° F. The temperature is lower at higher altitudes.

BOILED DRESSING—The name traditionally given to a homemade cooked salad dressing which is, in fact, not boiled at all. The dressing is low in fat and thickened with egg. It is made by cooking a white sauce-egg base to which vinegar, butter or margarine, and seasonings are added. It may be used with either fruits or vegetables. (See also *Salad Dressing*.)

BOMBAY DUCK—A slim, white, ocean fish of the Indian Ocean, whose real name is bummalo. The fish, about the size of a smelt, is dried and salted to be used as an accompaniment for curries. In parts of India it is served fried or curried. Canned Bombay duck is found in specialty stores.

BOMBE—A rich frozen layered dessert made with different flavored ice creams and/or sherbets and sometimes centered with mousse or whipped cream. The dessert is frozen in a special, fancy mold that can be tightly sealed. Bombe molds generally have lids, but a salad mold or metal mixing bowl can be used successfully when covered with foil. If freezer space is not available, the bombe may be frozen by burying the tightly sealed mold in a mixture of rock salt and ice for several hours. (See also *Frozen Dessert*.)

Raspberry Bombe

- 3 pints red raspberry sherbet
- 2 pints pink peppermint or strawberry ice cream
- 1 cup whipping cream
- 3 tablespoons confectioners' sugar
- ¼ cup finely chopped mixed candied fruits and peels
- ¼ cup finely chopped almonds, toasted
- Rum flavoring to taste

Chill a 2½-quart metal mold in freezer. Stir sherbet just to soften. With chilled spoon quickly spread over bottom and up the sides of mold; be sure sherbet comes to top. (If it slips, refreeze in mold till workable.) Freeze firm.

Stir the ice cream just to soften. Quickly spread over raspberry layer, covering completely. Freeze firm. Whip cream with sugar and dash salt to soft peaks. Fold in fruits, nuts, and flavoring. Pile into center of mold, smoothing top. Cover with foil; freeze 6 hours or overnight. Peel off foil. Invert mold on chilled plate. Rub mold with hot damp towel to loosen; lift off mold. Serves 12 to 16.

Brandied Bombe

- ¼ cup brandy
- 1 16-ounce can pitted dark sweet cherries, drained
- 1 quart vanilla ice cream
- 1 quart chocolate ice cream

Pour brandy over cherries and let stand 4 to 6 hours. Soften vanilla ice cream; mold to form shell about ¾ inch thick in a 5½-cup melon mold or a 1½-quart bowl. Freeze firm. Soften chocolate ice cream. Stir in cherries and brandy. Spoon into vanilla shell. Cover; freeze firm. Unmold. Decorate with pink-tinted whipped cream and chocolate curls, if desired. Makes 8 to 10 servings.

BONBON—The French term for any candy. In the United States it means a cream-centered candy coated in fondant. Sometimes fruit or nuts are added to the centers. The outside fondant may be tinted or flavored. (See also *Candy*.)

BONITO *(buh nē' tō)*—A saltwater fish related to the mackerel and tuna. Bonitos are caught in the Atlantic and Pacific oceans. They are sold fresh only in coastal areas. The majority are canned as chunks and flakes and used in salads and casseroles. (See also *Mackerel.*)

BONNE FEMME *(bôn fam)*—A descriptive term for a simple, home-style way of preparing food. *Bonne Femme,* a French phrase, means "a good obliging woman."

BORAGE *(bûr' ij, bôr' -)*—An herb which has a light cucumber flavor. The hairy leaves and stems are used in salads and to flavor cold beverages, especially punches and iced tea. The blue-star flowers are crystallized and used to decorate cakes.

Borage, a native of southern Europe, first became known as a cure for melancholy. The ancient Greeks put it in wine to bring good cheer. (See also *Herb.*)

BORDEAUX *(bôr dō')*—1. Name of city and wine growing region in southwestern France. 2. The wines from this region. Familiar varieties are Clarets, Sauternes, and Graves. (See *Claret, Sauterne, Wines and Spirits* for additional information.)

BORDELAISE *(bôr' duh lāz')*—A brown sauce for meat. Made with brown stock, red wine, and shallots and garnished with poached marrow and parsley, this sauce is good to serve with beef. (See also *Sauce.*)

Bordelaise Sauce

An elegant sauce to serve with beef—

Cook ½ cup sliced fresh mushrooms and 2 tablespoons chopped shallots in 1 tablespoon butter or margarine till tender. Blend 2 cups cooled beef stock into 3 tablespoons cornstarch; stir into mushroom-shallot mixture. Cook and stir till mixture boils. Stir in ¼ cup dry red wine; 1 tablespoon lemon juice; 2 teaspoons dried tarragon leaves, crushed; and dash pepper. Bring to boiling; reduce heat and simmer 5 to 10 minutes. Garnish with parsley or poached marrow, if desired. Makes about 2¼ cups sauce.

BORSCH, BORSCHT *(bôrsh, bôrsht)*—A beet soup of eastern European origin, primarily from Russia and Poland. There are several types of *borsch.* Some are made with meat or meat stock and others are made with vegetables, such as cabbage, but beets are always a principal ingredient. *Borsch* is eaten either hot or cold and may be served with sour cream. (See also *Soup.*)

Russian Borsch

2 cups shredded fresh beets
1 cup chopped carrots
1 cup chopped onion
1 10½-ounce can condensed beef broth
1 soup can water
1 cup coarsely chopped cabbage
1 tablespoon butter or margarine
1 tablespoon lemon juice
  Dairy sour cream

Combine beets, carrots, onion, and 2⅔ cups boiling salted water in large saucepan; cook covered 20 minutes. Add broth, water, cabbage, and butter; cook uncovered 15 minutes. Stir in lemon juice. Serve hot or chilled. Top with sour cream. Makes 6 to 8 servings.

BOSTON BROWN BREAD—A sweet, dark brown bread which is cooked by steaming. This bread is made with molasses for sweetening; combinations of cornmeal, rye meal, graham flour, and wheat flour; and, sometimes, dried fruit and nuts. Boston brown bread is traditionally served with baked beans. (See also *Bread.*)

Boston Brown Bread

1 cup sifted all-purpose flour
1 teaspoon baking powder
1 teaspoon baking soda
1 teaspoon salt
1 cup yellow cornmeal
1 cup stirred whole wheat flour

• • •

¾ cup dark molasses
2 cups buttermilk *or* sour milk
1 cup raisins

Ladle Bordelaise Sauce over a large steak which has been browned on the grill. To complement the mouth-watering steak, add crisp onion rings, salad, mugs of coffee, and fruit pie.

Sift all-purpose flour with baking powder, soda, and salt; stir in cornmeal and whole wheat flour. Add molasses, buttermilk, and raisins; beat well. Thoroughly clean four 16-ounce food cans. Grease and flour cans. Divide bread batter equally between the cans. Cover tops of cans tightly with foil.

Place on rack in deep kettle; pour in boiling water to 1-inch depth. Cover kettle; steam 3 hours, adding more boiling water, if needed. Uncover cans; bake at 450° for 5 minutes. Remove bread from cans. Cool on rack. Wrap and store overnight. Makes 4 loaves.

BOSTON BUTT—A cut of pork also known as Fresh Boston Shoulder. This meat cut contains a part of the blade bone and is suitable for roasting. Boston butt is made

Slicing circles of Boston Brown Bread is no trick when the bread is steamed in cans. Each can is greased and floured, filled with batter, and covered with aluminum foil.

into a smoked shoulder roll (butt) when the blade bone is removed and the largest muscle is cured and smoked. Roast or cook this cut in liquid. (See also *Pork*.)

Smoked Pork Dinner

1 2-pound smoked shoulder roll (butt)
   Prepared mustard
1 onion, sliced
1 17-ounce can vacuum packed sweet potatoes
¼ cup brown sugar
¼ cup butter or margarine, melted

Place pork in Dutch oven; cover with cold water and bring just to a boil. Simmer 2 hours or till tender. Remove from water. Slice; spread with mustard. Place meat and onion slices alternately in 13x9x2-inch baking dish.

Arrange potatoes around edges; top with brown sugar and drizzle butter over top. Bake, covered, at 350° for 1 hour. Uncover and bake 30 minutes longer. Makes 8 servings.

BOSTON CREAM PIE—A dessert which is made of cake, despite the name "pie." Two layers of sponge or white cake are stacked together with a thick cream or custard filling in the middle. Chocolate frosting or confectioners' sugar is spread over the top. Washington Pie is similar, but has jam or jelly between the layers. (See also *Cake*.)

Boston Cream Pie

1 2-inch piece vanilla bean *or*
   1½ teaspoons vanilla extract
1 cup milk
2 egg whites
½ cup sugar
   • • •
2¼ cups sifted cake flour
1 cup sugar
3 teaspoons baking powder
1 teaspoon salt
⅓ cup salad oil
2 egg yolks
   Custard Filling
   Chocolate Glaze

Slit vanilla bean and remove seed. Add bean to milk; let stand 3 hours. Remove bean; discard. *Or* add vanilla extract to milk. Beat egg whites to soft peaks; gradually add ½ cup sugar, beating till very stiff and glossy.

Sift flour, 1 cup sugar, baking powder, and salt together into another bowl. Add oil and *half* the milk to dry mixture; beat 1 minute at medium speed on mixer, scraping bowl frequently. Add remaining milk and egg yolks. Beat 1 minute more. Fold in egg white mixture.

Pour batter into 2 paper-lined 9x1½-inch round cake pans; bake at 350° for 25 to 30 minutes. Cool slightly; remove from pans. Cool. Spread one layer with Custard Filling. Place second cake layer on custard and glaze.

Custard Filling: Combine ⅓ cup sugar, 2 tablespoons all-purpose flour, 1 tablespoon cornstarch, and ¼ teaspoon salt. Gradually add 1½ cups milk; mix well. Cook and stir over medium heat till thickened and bubbly; cook 2 to 3 minutes more. Beat together 1 egg and 1 egg yolk; stir a little of the hot mixture into egg; return to hot mixture. Cook and stir till mixture boils. Stir in 1 teaspoon vanilla. Cover surface with waxed paper; cool. Spread filling over first cake layer.

Chocolate Glaze: Place one 1-ounce square unsweetened chocolate and 1 tablespoon butter or margarine in small saucepan. Stir over low heat till melted. Remove from heat; add 1 cup sifted confectioners' sugar and ½ teaspoon vanilla. Blend in enough boiling water to make glaze soft enough to spread. Spread the chocolate glaze over top of second cake layer.

Bite into this Boston Cream Pie, a luscious combination of creamy filling between layers of cake, topped-off with a chocolate glaze.

Boston Lettuce is distinguished by soft-textured, light green outer leaves. Inner leaves are light yellow and feel oily.

BOSTON LETTUCE—A sweet, delicate lettuce sometimes called "Butterhead." The heads are softer and the leaves are not as crisp as Iceberg lettuce. Large Boston leaves are brown on the edge. Select heads that are fairly firm with fresh, soft leaves. Store Boston lettuce in a plastic bag in crisper of the refrigerator for one or two days. (See also *Lettuce.*)

BOTULISM *(boch' uh liz' uhm)*—A type of food poisoning caused by eating spoiled foods, usually found in meat, fish, and canned foods which have been inadequately sterilized. A trace can be fatal. Because botulism cannot be detected by any taste, spoiled canned foods, bulging cans, and leaky cans should be discarded without tasting. (See also *Food Poisoning.*)

BOUCHEE *(boo sha')*—1. Small patty shell or puff pastry. 2. A type of petit four.

Bouchees are baked blind and then filled with a creamy mixture. Fish and meat combinations are used for hot hors d'oeuvres and sweet fillings for desserts.

Petits fours, known as brochees, are usually made commercially. These dainty sweets are chocolates with a filled center. Nougat, praline, toffee, and liqueur are often used for fillings. (See also *Puff Pastry.*)

BOUILLABAISSE *(bool' yuh bas', bool' yuh bas')*—A pungent soup or stew made with several kinds of fish and shellfish. As many as seven or eight kinds of fish are cooked with water or white wine, olive oil, tomatoes, saffron, garlic, and herbs.

The true bouillabaisse is considered to be the type originated in Marseille, France. However, legend attributes its invention to Venus, the beguiling goddess, who prepared it for her husband to induce sound sleep. (See also *Soup.*)

Bouillabaisse Soup

½ pound fresh shrimp in shells
½ pound codfish
½ pound scallops
6 oysters
2 tablespoons minced onion
1 clove garlic, minced
2 tablespoons minced celery
2 tablespoons minced green pepper
½ cup butter or margarine
½ cup all-purpose flour
1 cup cooked lobster (1½ pounds whole or 1 medium lobster tail)

Shell and clean shrimp, saving shells. Tie codfish in cheesecloth; place codfish, scallops, shrimp, oysters, and 1 teaspoon salt in 2 quarts water; bring to boil. Reduce heat, simmer 5 minutes; drain, reserving stock. Place shrimp shells in reserved stock and cook till liquid is reduced to 4 cups.

Strain stock through a cheesecloth. Cook onion, garlic, celery, and green pepper in butter till tender. Add flour, then stir in 2 cups stock; cook and stir till thickened.

Dice codfish, scallops, shrimp, and lobster; add to thickened soup with oysters; heat through. (Refrigerate remaining fish stock for future use.) Makes 4 to 6 servings.

BOUILLON *(bool' yon, -yuhn)*—Clear, seasoned broth. Beef, chicken, fish, or vegetables are cooked in water to extract the flavor and then the liquid is strained. Bouillon cubes or granules may also be dissolved in hot water to make the broth.

Bouillon may be used to flavor dishes or served by itself as a beverage or soup.

BOUQUET (*bō kā' boo-*)—The distinctive fragrance of wines and liqueurs. Chemical reactions during the fermentation and aging process produce this fragrance. The bouquet should have a "clean" smell with no hint of moldiness. It may be rather faint when the bottle is first opened or when cold. (See also *Wines and Spirits*.)

BOUQUET GARNI (*bō kā' gär nē'*)—A bundle of herbs, basically made with thyme, parsley, and bay leaf. Other herbs, such as basil, celery, garlic, marjoram, and rosemary, are added depending on the nature of the food that will be seasoned. These herbs are tied together, usually in a cheesecloth bag, and simmered in a stew, soup, or sauce. The bouquet garni is removed before the food is served, an easy process because the herbs are bundled together and do not need straining. (See also *Herbs*.)

Bouquet Garni

    3 or 4 sprigs parsley
    1 medium bay leaf
    ¼ teaspoon dried thyme leaves *or*
        1 teaspoon fresh thyme
    2 or 3 sprigs celery leaves

Place all ingredients in tea ball or cheesecloth bag. Simmer in soup, stew, or sauce; remove from food before serving.

BOUQUETIERE (*buk' tje*) — A vegetable garnish used on meat dishes.

BOURBON—A whiskey distilled from corn. Bourbon was first made in Bourbon County, Kentucky, in 1782 by Elijah Craig, a Baptist minister.

The name bourbon is given to whiskey distilled from fermented mash of grain and distilled at not more than 160° proof. The grain must be at least 51 percent corn; other grains, such as rye and malt, are used for the balance. New charred oak barrels are required to age the whiskey.

Most bourbon is labeled Straight Bourbon or Blended Straight Bourbon. Straight is heavy, dry, mellow and full-bodied. Blended, a blend of straights, is lighter.

Corn whiskey which contains at least 80 percent corn and aged in used containers, if aged at all, is not to be confused with bourbon. (See also *Whiskey*.)

BOURGUIGNONNE (*boor' gen yun'*) — A method of preparing food which originated in the Burgundy region of France. Beef, especially large cuts, poultry, fish, and eggs are prepared with a red wine sauce and garnished with mushrooms and onions.

BOYSENBERRY—A hybrid fruit developed by crossing varieties of blackberries and raspberries. The fruit resembles a blackberry with a flavor like that of the raspberry. Boysenberry is named for Rudolph Boysen, the twentieth-century American who developed it. (See also *Berry*.)

BRAINS—The edible brain from beef, veal, pork, and lamb. This mild-flavored variety meat has a soft consistency which makes it an easy food to digest.

Brains are highly perishable, therefore select only fresh ones which have a bright color. Refrigerate and use within 24 hours. If brains are precooked, they can be stored for 48 hours. One pound will make approximately four servings.

Wash brains under running water or soak in cold water and vinegar solution for 30 minutes. Drain; remove membrane and blood particles from the meat.

Precooking is not essential but does improve texture, flavor, and increases the storage time. Precook by covering with salted water and simmering 20 to 30 minutes; drain and chill in cold water.

Use precooked brains immediately or refrigerate and prepare later. Brains are served broiled, fried, braised, or cooked with another food, such as scrambled eggs or a sauce. (See also *Variety Meat*.)

Deep-Fried Brains

    1 pound brains (about 2)
        Vinegar *or* lemon juice
    1 slightly beaten egg
    1 tablespoon milk
    1 cup finely crushed saltine
        cracker crumbs

Simmer brains 20 minutes in water to which 1 tablespoon vinegar *or* lemon juice and 1 teaspoon salt have been added for each quart water. Drain. Remove membrane, if any, and cut brains in half lengthwise.

Combine egg and milk. Dip brains into egg mixture, then in crumbs. Fry in deep hot fat (360°) about 2 minutes or till crisp and brown. Serve with tartar sauce. Serves 4.

BRAISE—To cook by browning slowly in hot shortening and then simmering in a small amount of liquid. The meat can be coated with flour before browning, if desired. Wine, stock, bouillon, or water may be added for the liquid. Cooking is continued in a tightly covered pan placed in a slow oven or over low heat on top of the range.

This moist-heat method of cooking is suitable for less-tender cuts of meat because the long, slow cooking with moisture breaks down the connective tissue.

Sweet-Sour Lamb Chops

    4 lamb shoulder chops, about
        1 inch thick
 ¼ cup brown sugar
 ¼ cup vinegar
 ½ teaspoon ground ginger
    4 orange slices
    4 lemon wedges
    1 tablespoon cornstarch

In skillet brown chops on both sides in small amount of hot shortening. Combine sugar, vinegar, 1 teaspoon salt, ginger, and dash pepper; pour over meat. Top each with orange and lemon piece. Cover; cook over low heat 30 minutes or till tender. Remove to platter.

Skim fat off pan juices. Add water to make 1 cup. Blend cornstarch with 1 tablespoon cold water; stir into liquid in skillet. Cook, stirring constantly, till mixture thickens and bubbles. Serve sauce over lamb chops on hot cooked rice, if desired. Makes 4 servings.

Braise Sweet-Sour Lamb Chops in a brown sugar and vinegar sauce which is spiked with ginger. Tangy, translucent orange and lemon slices accent the flavor while garnishing the chops.

BRAN—The coarse, outer layer of a grain kernel. During the milling of grains into flour, such as wheat or rice, the entire kernel is ground. The bran layer flakes into particles larger than the flour and is separated by sifting or bolting. Bran, composed of several thin layers with a papery structure, is made into cereals and flour or sold as animal feed.

To make bran into ready-to-eat cereal, it is cooked and rolled into crisp flakes. These cereals may be either 100 percent bran or a combination of bran, usually 40 percent, with another part of a grain kernel. Flour made with the entire kernel is called whole wheat or graham flour.

Ready-to-eat cereals are eaten as a breakfast food and used as an ingredient. Cookies, breads, muffins, meat loaves, and stuffings made with either bran cereal or flour have a wholesome flavor and aroma.

Bran, a carbohydrate, is composed of cellulose which gives bulk to the diet. As bran has a high laxative action, use discrimination when eating it, and when giving it to children. Too much can be irritating to the system. Minerals and B vitamins (riboflavin, niacin, and thiamine) are naturally found in bran, but may also be added to enrich it or to restore those removed in processing. (See also *Grain*.)

Spread Apricot Bran Bread with butter or margarine curls for a snack or with cream cheese to serve with a soup or salad lunch.

Apricot Bran Bread

    1 cup finely snipped dried
        apricots
    3 tablespoons sugar
 1½ cups sifted all-purpose flour
    ½ cup sugar
 3¾ teaspoons baking powder
    1 teaspoon salt
 1½ cups whole bran cereal
    1 cup milk
    2 beaten eggs
    ⅓ cup salad oil

Pour enough boiling water over apricots to cover; let stand 10 minutes. Drain well; combine apricots and 3 tablespoons sugar.

Sift together flour, ½ cup sugar, baking powder, and salt. Mix bran cereal, milk, eggs, and oil; add to flour mixture, stirring just till moistened. Gently stir in apricot mixture. Turn into greased 9x5x3-inch loaf pan. Sprinkle top with a little sugar. Bake in 350° oven for 1 hour. Remove from pan; cool on rack.

Cheddar Bran Muffins

    1 cup whole bran
 1¼ cups buttermilk *or* sour milk
    ¼ cup shortening
    ⅓ cup sugar
    1 egg
        • • •
 1½ cups sifted all-purpose flour
 1½ teaspoons baking powder
    ½ teaspoon salt
    ¼ teaspoon baking soda
    4 ounces sharp Cheddar cheese
        shredded (1 cup)

Soften bran in buttermilk. Cream shortening and sugar till fluffy; beat in egg. Sift together flour, baking powder, salt, and soda. Add to creamed mixture alternately with bran mixture. Stir in cheese. Fill greased muffin pans ⅔ full. Bake at 400° for 30 minutes. Serve warm. Makes 1 dozen bran muffins.

BRANDIED—To be soaked or flavored with brandy as when a brandy syrup is poured over fruits or desserts. The syrup enriches their flavor and texture.